WOMEN'S RIGHT TO VOTE

HISTORY SMASHERS

The Mayflower

Women's Right to Vote

WOMEN'S RIGHT TO VOTE

KATE MESSNER

ILLUSTRATED BY DYLAN MECONIS

With special thanks to Olugbemisola Rhuday-Perkovich,
who served as a consultant and contributor for this book

RANDOM HOUSE 🏠 NEW YORK

Text copyright © 2020 by Kate Messner
Cover art and interior illustrations copyright © 2020 by Dylan Meconis

All rights reserved. Published in the United States by Random House Children's Books, a division of Penguin Random House LLC, New York.

Random House and the colophon are registered trademarks of Penguin Random House LLC.

Visit us on the Web! rhcbooks.com

Educators and librarians, for a variety of teaching tools, visit us at RHTeachersLibrarians.com

Library of Congress Cataloging-in-Publication Data
Names: Messner, Kate, author. | Meconis, Dylan, illustrator.
Title: Women's right to vote / Kate Messner; illustrated by Dylan Meconis.
Description: New York: Random House Children's Books, 2020. | Series: History smashers | Includes bibliographical references and index. | Audience: Ages 8–12
Identifiers: LCCN 2019031526 | ISBN 978-0-593-12034-7 (trade paperback) | ISBN 978-0-593-12035-4 (lib. bdg.) | ISBN 978-0-593-12036-1 (ebook)
Subjects: LCSH: Women—Suffrage—United States—History—Juvenile literature. | United States. Constitution. 19th Amendment—History—Juvenile literature.
Classification: LCC JK1898 .M47 2020 | DDC 324.6/230973—dc23

Printed in the United States of America
10 9 8 7 6 5 4 3 2 1
First Edition

*For all who fought for
voting rights, and for those
who continue the fight today*

CONTENTS

You've probably heard stories about how American women won the right to vote. Chances are, you learned about Susan B. Anthony, who fought for that right along with some of her friends.

It's true that for a long time in America, only men could vote. That went on for more than a hundred years, until women got so angry that they did something about it. Maybe this is where you've imagined Susan B. Anthony and her pals coming into the story—a group of women in fancy hats, drinking tea, writing letters, and talking about equality. But that's just a tiny part of what happened.

The true story about women's right to vote is a lot longer and more complicated than that. And Susan B. Anthony was just a part of that bigger picture—a story of women who worked together but also fought with one another. They argued over everything from who should get to vote to how they should go about making change.

Sometimes those women had one another's backs, and sometimes they didn't. Some of the same white women who talked and wrote about justice and equality fought hard to keep women of color living separate and unequal lives. Sometimes the women who fought for voting rights were heroes—and sometimes not so much. Some of them worked hard to hide the contributions of other heroes because of the color of their skin. In the end, the story of women's fight for the right to vote is a much messier one than history books like to share. Let's smash that old story! Here's the real deal. . . .

ONE
WHO IS A CITIZEN?

Today it's hard to imagine how anyone could argue that some Americans should get to vote while others shouldn't. To understand the fight for voting rights, you have to understand that for the European men who colonized America, inequality was a tradition. Most of those early colonists came from England, where married women weren't even allowed to own property. Everything those women owned before they got married suddenly belonged to their husbands after the wedding.

In England, you had to be a man who owned property in order to vote. The colonists brought that system with them when they settled on the other side of the ocean. The men who wrote America's founding documents, the Declaration of Independence and the Constitution, held on to those old ideas when they set up the new nation's government. The only real discussion of women's rights at that time came from their wives.

As America was getting ready to declare its independence from Great Britain in 1776, Abigail Adams raised the issue in a letter to her husband, future-president John Adams.

In the new code of laws which I suppose it will be necessary for you to make, I desire you would remember the ladies and be more generous and favorable to them than your ancestors.

It's probably no surprise to you that John ignored Abigail's advice. Eleven years later, he and the other men in charge of the new nation sat down to write the US Constitution, the document that would outline how the government would work. They spent weeks debating what should be included, but they never even talked about the possibility of women voting. For the men in that room, that just wasn't how things worked.

Before the Revolutionary War, individual colonies had all kinds of different laws about who could vote and who couldn't. Sometimes it was based on race. In much of the South, where many Black people were enslaved, even free Black men weren't allowed to vote. You had to be male *and* white. Native American men were allowed to vote in some colonies but not others. And in some places, voting rights depended on religion.

When the colonies broke away from England, the new states made their own rules about who could vote.

Some decided to stick with tradition, giving the vote to men who owned a certain amount of property. Other states changed things up a little. In New Jersey, men could vote if they had *either* fifty pounds' worth of property or money. Vermont decided to let all men vote, whether they owned anything or not.

When it was time to figure out voting rights on the national level, the men who wrote the Constitution talked about including a property rule. Some lawmakers loved that idea. They were mostly from the South, where men who owned lots of property wanted to keep power for themselves. But others argued that men who didn't own property were already voting in some states. If the Constitution included a property requirement, they'd lose a right they already had. That didn't seem fair at all.

As the men talked, two very different ideas about voting emerged. Some said voting was **a privilege you should have to earn** . . . somehow. (Usually by having enough money to own property.) Others argued that voting was **a natural right** that should be given to all people, and that it couldn't—or shouldn't—be taken away by anyone.

The committee argued about this question for more than a week during the hot, sticky summer of 1787. Finally the men reached an agreement. They decided . . . not to make a decision. They left the issue of who gets to vote out of the Constitution entirely. The original document never mentions gender or property requirements. It only explains that under the new government, "people" would choose their representatives.

Not people who own property.

Not men.

Just people.

At first you might think that sounds great. There are no restrictions on voting in the Constitution! Everybody gets to vote! Right?

Wrong.

The way the Constitution is set up, everything that's *not* a national law is left up to the states. So when it came to voting rights, each state could decide who counted as a "person" in that state, and who got to vote. If your state decided you were person enough to vote in state elections, you could vote in national elections, too. If not, then you didn't get a say in how your country was run, either.

It probably won't surprise you to learn that wealthy white men counted as "people" in every state. Free Black men were most often considered "people" in the North but not in the South. And with the exception of New Jersey for a short time, women weren't "people" anywhere.

It turns out that the Constitution, the original set of rules for America's democracy, did little to make sure everyone would have a voice in the new government. In leaving the language so vague, the men who wrote the Constitution didn't really guarantee voting rights for anyone. Instead, they set the stage for battles that would rage on for decades . . . and that are still happening today.

HOW WOMEN VOTED IN NEW JERSEY ... UNTIL THEY COULDN'T

When the new states set up laws about who could vote, women were banned from the polls *almost* everywhere. The one exception was New Jersey. There, the state constitution said "all inhabitants" of the colony could vote, as long as they were old enough and owned fifty pounds' worth of property. No one knows for sure why New Jersey didn't specify that only men could vote, as in the other states. Was it an accident? Or did the state mean for women to vote? There *were* lots of Quakers in New Jersey, and Quakers believe in the equality of all people.

Whatever the reason, women noticed the language in the state constitution. It didn't say they *couldn't* vote. So some of them showed up and voted. No one bothered them, and everything was fine for a while.

But as time passed, some men decided they didn't like the idea of women voting after all. They complained that the women who showed up at the polls weren't very ladylike. The men also had concerns about women getting too much power. What if they decided to vote all together on an issue? They could have a real influence on elections. So in 1807, New Jersey's lawmakers passed a law that said women couldn't vote anymore. Can you guess how many women had a say in that decision? None. All the lawmakers were men. With that vote, New Jersey's women lost their right to vote and didn't get it back for over a hundred years.

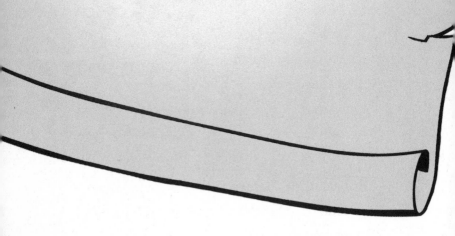

TWO

IT ALL STARTED IN SENECA FALLS . . . OR DID IT?

The sleepy town of Seneca Falls, New York, is sometimes called the birthplace of the women's rights movement. Maybe you've heard of the convention that happened there in 1848 and launched the movement for woman suffrage, or voting rights.

But if you heard that Seneca Falls was the start of the whole thing, you haven't heard the real deal.

The idea of women having power in government felt new to

WELCOME TO
HISTORIC
SENECA FALLS
ESTABLISHED
1831

BIRTHPLACE OF
WOMEN'S RIGHTS

American women. But it wasn't really a new idea at all. Women had held leadership positions all over the world. In Africa, that tradition went back centuries. In the 1500s, Queen Amina ruled (and commanded an army!) in what is now called Nigeria. Some European monarchs were women, too. Queen Victoria was ruling the United Kingdom at the time of that first women's rights convention in America.

Amina
ruled
1576–1610

Victoria
ruled
1876–1901

The village of Seneca Falls was built on the traditional lands of the Haudenosaunee people. Haudenosaunee women had always had a say in their communities. As clan mothers, they had—and still have—the responsibility of nominating and advising the chiefs.

And long before English Pilgrims settled in the territory of the Wampanoag people, in what's now called Massachusetts, Wampanoag women played major roles in making tribal decisions. They could even become the important leaders called sachems.

Weetamoo was a Pocasset Wampanoag woman who took over as sachem after her husband Wamsutta died in 1662. (There's evidence to suggest that the English poisoned Wamsutta while he was visiting them.)

Women who lived in England and the United States had none of those rights. And they started speaking up about it way before that convention in Seneca Falls.

Mary Wollstonecraft was a teacher and activist who fought for change in England. She thought women and men should have the same opportunities when it came to education. In 1792, she wrote an official document outlining her beliefs.

Some of the first American women to speak up in the 1800s wanted rights for themselves so they could fight for the rights of others. Even though the Declaration of Independence had declared all men equal, it was legal to keep people enslaved, with no pay and no freedom. Antislavery activists spoke up about how wrong that was, and some of those activists were women.

Wherever those women went, people criticized them for giving talks. Women were expected to be quiet and agreeable. They weren't supposed to run around giving speeches in front of audiences that included men. It was a scandal!

All that criticism made the women feel prickly. Men were allowed to speak up about slavery. Why shouldn't they? They were trying to do good work in the world. Why were people giving them such a hard time?

You might think those women got frustrated and called it a day, but that's not what happened. They kept giving talks against slavery. They also started speaking out about something else—their own rights to give public speeches.

Two sisters named Sarah and Angelina Grimké had a lot to say about this. They were from South Carolina and thought it was awful that their family enslaved people. So they moved to Philadelphia and gave antislavery talks.

When people criticized the Grimkés for that, the sisters fought back and defended their rights. Sarah

Sarah Grimké   Angelina Grimké

Grimké even wrote a newspaper series about women's rights.

Abby Kelley Foster, a Quaker woman from Massachusetts, was giving antislavery talks around the same time—and facing all the same problems. People mocked her. They threw rotten fruit and eggs at her. Once, protesters even burned down a building where she'd just given a talk.

You might think that would convince Abby Kelley Foster to take a break, but it just fired her up. She figured if people were that ignorant, she had a lot of work to do. So she started speaking up for women's rights, too.

Abby Kelley Foster

These conversations were already in the air when a young woman named Elizabeth Cady Stanton traveled with her new husband, Henry, to London. Henry was attending the World Anti-Slavery Convention there. Elizabeth wasn't an activist yet. She was just going along to watch. On that trip she met Lucretia Mott, a well-known antislavery activist.

Mott and other women had traveled across the ocean to be part of the convention. But when the meeting started, all those women were banned from speaking. The men in charge argued about it for a while. They decided to let the women sit in the back, where they could listen as long as they didn't talk. A few of the men understood how unfair that was. They chose to sit in back with the women as a form of protest.

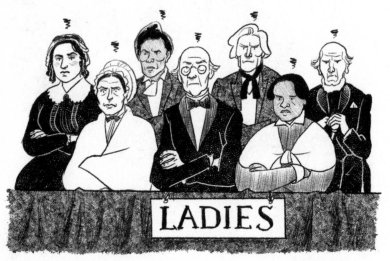

LADIES

Lucretia Mott had spent a lot of time working in the antislavery movement. She was used to being treated poorly by men, so while she wasn't happy about this, she wasn't surprised, either. But Elizabeth Cady Stanton was outraged. Later she wrote about how angry she was. She described how she and Mott had vowed to work together on a women's rights convention when they got home. This story became a big part of the myth of that Seneca Falls convention. Lucretia Mott never mentioned any of this in her diary, though, so we only know Stanton's version of the story.

LUCRETIA MOTT'S BOYCOTT

The seeds for Lucretia Mott's life as an anti-slavery activist were planted when she was a little girl and saw an enslaved woman being whipped in the center of her town. She was so upset. How could anyone treat another person that way?

Lucretia Mott was from a family of Quakers who believed in equality. She learned more about the slave trade in school. Later, she took a trip to Virginia, where she saw en-slaved people working in the fields. That's when she promised to stop using any products produced by slave labor.

When a person refuses to buy or use goods for moral reasons, that's called a boycott. In this case, Lucretia Mott stopped using cotton, which was picked by people who were en-slaved. She gave up sugar and molasses, too. Instead, she bought her children sweets that were made without slave labor and handed them out with a special note.

Lucretia Mott started giving talks about her boycott. She became a Quaker minister and eventually founded the Pennsylvania Anti-Slavery Society and the Philadelphia Female Anti-Slavery Society.

In 1846, Elizabeth Cady Stanton moved from Boston to Seneca Falls with her family. Her husband traveled a lot. Before long, she felt bored and frustrated with all the housework she had to do.

Stanton was complaining about this to her friends when they got together for tea one day in July 1848. Lucretia Mott was visiting the area, so she was there, too. Whether or not they'd ever talked about it before, now the ladies decided it was time to hold a convention about women's rights. They took out an ad in the newspaper to invite people.

Women's Rights Convention.

A Convention to discuss the social, civil and religious condition and rights of Woman, will be held in the Wesleyan Chapel, at Seneca Falls, N. Y., on Wednesday and Thursday the 19th and 20th of July current, commencing at 10 o'clock A. M.

During the first day, the meeting will be exclusively for Women, which all are earnestly invited to attend. The public generally are invited to be present on the second day, when LUCRETIA MOTT, of Philadelphia, and others both ladies and gentlemen, will address the Convention.

The women wrote a document they called the Declaration of Sentiments. They used the Declaration of Independence as a model. They changed the line about all men being equal to read "all men and women are created equal." The rest of the document listed their demands.

ACCESS TO EDUCATION
PROPERTY RIGHTS
EQUALITY AT WORK AND AT HOME
VOTING RIGHTS

Three hundred people showed up for the convention. It was a pretty great turnout for something planned with just eight days' notice! At this point, you're probably imagining Elizabeth Cady Stanton and Lucretia Mott up in front of the chapel, chairing the meeting they called. It was their idea, so they'd run the whole show, right?

Wrong.

Convention organizers worried that people would criticize them if they had a woman in front of the crowd, so they planned for Lucretia's husband, James, to serve as chair. He ended up being too sick to come on the first day, but he ran things on day two, when men were there, too.

Mott was supportive of the women's goals, which is more than we can say for Elizabeth Cady Stanton's husband, who left town on the day of the convention.

For two days, people listened to speakers and took turns sharing ideas about the Declaration of Sentiments. On the first day, only women spoke. On the second day, men were part of the discussion, too. Then it was time for everyone to vote on the resolutions included in that document. Most people liked all the resolutions except this one:

RESOLVED, THAT IS IT THE DUTY OF THE WOMEN OF THIS COUNTRY TO SECURE TO THEMSELVES THEIR SACRED RIGHT TO THE ELECTIVE FRANCHISE.

In other words: Women should demand the right to vote.

That resolution was so controversial that even Lucretia Mott suggested getting rid of it. But

Elizabeth Cady Stanton argued that women *needed* the right to vote. Without it, they wouldn't have power to make anything change at all.

Frederick Douglass backed her up on that. Douglass, who had once been enslaved, was a well-known antislavery speaker in Rochester, New York. He was highly respected among activists, and historians think it was probably his support that saved the resolution about voting.

So just how important was this convention? The truth is, nothing really changed on that day. No new laws were made. It wasn't the first time women had spoken up about equality or demanded voting rights. But it *was* the first time American women had called a big meeting just for that purpose. Newspapers wrote about that, and people talked about it, too.

The National Reformer

AUGUST 3, 1848

WOMEN'S RIGHTS CONVENTION

Right away people started planning more conventions. Activists held one in Rochester, New York, the following month. And a woman actually got to run that meeting! When Abigail Bush headed up that convention, she became the first woman ever to run a public meeting with both men and women in the United States.

WHO WEARS THE PANTS?

Women didn't just fight for the right to vote. They spoke up about other issues, too—including the right to make their own clothing choices. At that time, women were expected to wear long, puffy skirts. Only men wore pants. But women had noticed that pants seemed easier to move around in than those heavy, fancy skirts.

So Amelia Bloomer, who had attended the Seneca Falls convention and published a newspaper that covered women's issues, made a fashion statement. She started wearing loose, baggy pants with shorter dresses—a fashion that came to be called bloomers. Other women started wearing them, too. But mostly people made fun of them. The mocking got so bad that eventually most women stopped wearing bloomers because the clothing took attention away from more important issues, like the right to vote.

Before long, conventions were springing up in other states, too. Women wondered what might happen if they had an even bigger meeting—one that included activists from the whole country.

In 1850, two early abolitionists and women's rights speakers, Abby Kelley Foster and Lucy Stone, got together in Boston to make plans for the first National Woman's Rights Convention. It took place in Worcester,

Massachusetts, that October. Some of the most famous antislavery and women's rights activists of the time were there. Frederick Douglass spoke. So did Sojourner Truth. Like Douglass, she had been enslaved and had come to speak up for her rights and the rights of others.

This meeting was controversial, too. Newspapers called the ladies who dared to share their views "unwomanly." But more than a thousand people from eleven states showed up and talked about the need for action. It became clear that no matter how many people said ladies should stick to baking pies and being quiet, that wasn't going to happen. The women kept getting louder, and the movement began to grow.

FRANCES ELLEN WATKINS HARPER

Frances Ellen Watkins Harper had a way with words. She wrote poems, short stories, news articles, and novels. Harper played an important role in the fight for women's right to vote. She argued that the white women fighting alongside her needed to pay more attention to issues of race in America.

YOU WHITE WOMEN SPEAK HERE OF RIGHTS. I SPEAK OF WRONGS. . . .

I TELL YOU THAT IF THERE IS ANY CLASS OF PEOPLE WHO NEED TO BE LIFTED OUT OF THEIR AIRY NOTHINGS AND SELFISHNESS, IT IS THE WHITE WOMEN OF AMERICA.

Harper was born to free parents in 1825. Her parents died when she was young, so her uncle and aunt raised her. Her uncle was a minister who spoke out against slavery. He ran the school she attended. That probably had a big influence on Harper's later work as a suffragist, civil rights advocate, and writer.

BURY ME IN A FREE LAND

Make me a grave where'er you will,
In a lowly plain, or a lofty hill;
Make it among earth's humblest graves,
But not in a land where men are slaves.

Harper believed the federal government should protect the rights of all citizens—not just white men. She tried to build partnerships with white suffragists who seemed to be fighting for the same causes, but with little success. Harper went on to help found the National Association of Colored Women with another activist, Mary Church Terrell.

INTERSECTIONAL FEMINISM

Today, we'd say that many of those white suffragists failed to be intersectional. In other
words, they didn't stop to consider how people
from backgrounds different from their own
might be affected by the issue.

A modern civil rights activist and scholar
named Kimberlé Williams Crenshaw was the
first to use the word "intersectional" in talking
about women's rights. She's given talks and
written extensively about how Black women
face discrimination because of their gender
and the color of their skin.

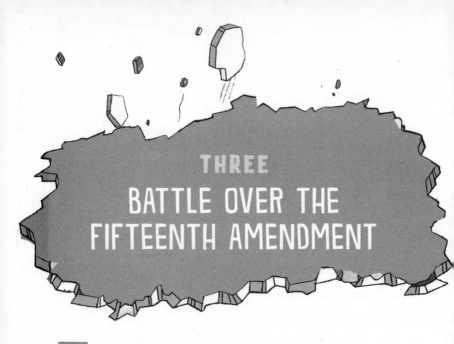

THREE
BATTLE OVER THE FIFTEENTH AMENDMENT

The push for women's equality and voting rights gained popularity after that first national convention in 1850. Women gave talks and wrote articles about equal rights. Women who could afford it launched their own newspapers to discuss the issues.

A PAPER DEVOTED TO THE ELEVATION OF WOMEN

DEVOTED TO THE INTERESTS OF WOMEN

There were more conventions, too—small ones in towns and villages, bigger ones at the state level, and every year another national gathering—where activists came together to talk.

But while this was happening, the issue of slavery was moving America closer to civil war. The Tenth National Woman's Rights Convention, held in 1860, was the last one before the Civil War broke out in April 1861.

At that point, women's rights activists put their projects on hold to support the war effort. They took over family farms. They worked in factories to fill in for the men who'd gone off to fight. They gathered food and medical supplies and helped care for injured soldiers.

Many women's rights activists spoke out against slavery, too. Elizabeth Cady Stanton and Lucy Stone worked together to support a new law that would abolish slavery. Susan B. Anthony, who'd starting going to conventions in the early 1850s, joined them. They set up a group called the Women's Loyal National League, which wrote a petition against slavery. Women traveled around collecting signatures until four hundred thousand people had signed it. The women delivered that petition to Washington, DC, hoping to outlaw slavery once and for all. But that would require a change to the Constitution.

How does that happen? The men who wrote the Constitution understood that over time the world would change, and it would be necessary to change America's founding document, too. But amending the Constitution is a long process. For an amendment to be added, it has to be voted on in both houses of Congress—the Senate and the House of Representatives—and it has to get two-thirds of the vote in each. Then the amendment has to be ratified, or approved, by three-quarters of the states.

HOW TO...*Amend the Constitution!*

STEP 1:
TWO-THIRDS MAJORITY
VOTE IN THE SENATE

STEP 2:
TWO-THIRDS MAJORITY VOTE IN
THE HOUSE OF REPRESENTATIVES

STEP 3: APPROVAL, OR RATIFICATION, BY
THREE-QUARTERS OF THE STATES

The Thirteenth Amendment—the one that bans slavery in the United States—made it through that whole process and was ratified in December 1865.

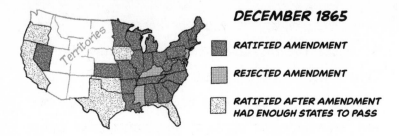

Then the women who'd been fighting for voting rights got back to work. Now that the war was over, they hoped the nation would recognize all the amazing work women had done and grant them the right to vote. But it didn't work out that way.

The women brought back their annual conventions with a meeting in New York City in May 1866. They formed a group called the American Equal Rights Association, or AERA, with Lucretia Mott as president. The group would fight for voting rights for all people, no matter their gender or race.

It seems like such a good idea, doesn't it? How could anyone argue that?

But as time went on, there were *lots* of arguments. Some came about because of two more proposed amendments to the Constitution. The Fourteenth Amendment, ratified in July 1868, said all people born or naturalized in the United States were citizens. That included people who had been enslaved but were free now. This might not seem controversial, but the amendment also said states couldn't deny voting rights "to any of the male inhabitants." The Constitution had never used the word "male" or "female" in talking about people's rights. But here, for the first time, it was clear that some rights were intended only for men.

TO ANY OF THE MALE INHABITANTS . . .

And then came the Fifteenth Amendment. It said states couldn't deny people the right to vote on the basis of "race, color, or previous condition of servitude." That last part was a reference to slavery. The amendment didn't mention gender, so discriminating against women was still fine.

People who supported the Fifteenth Amendment had good reasons to fight for it. After the Civil War, many states in the South imposed harsh laws that were designed to keep former slaves from really being free. Those laws, called Black Codes, restricted the freedom of African Americans and kept them working for white landowners for very low wages.

Many white people in the South were angry about the end of slavery. They did everything they could to maintain a society based on white supremacy, the idea that white people are superior to all other races and should rule over people of color. In the years after the Civil War, a time period we now call Reconstruction, white supremacist groups such as the Ku Klux Klan terrorized Black people. Many thousands of African Americans were threatened and beaten. Some were publicly and illegally murdered, often by mobs of whites, in gruesome ways called lynchings. The police most often did nothing to stop this from happening. Some of them even participated in the attacks. It was truly dangerous to be Black in the South. Something had to be done.

That's why so many activists fought for the Fifteenth Amendment. Their hope was that if Black men were guaranteed the right to vote, they'd be able to change those unfair laws. You might think that suffragists would understand how important that was.

After all, many of them had started out as abolitionists, fighting racial injustice. But the Fifteenth Amendment ended up causing arguments that ripped the woman suffrage movement apart.

Two of the most famous suffrage leaders, Elizabeth Cady Stanton and Susan B. Anthony, fiercely opposed the Fifteenth Amendment. They spoke out against it every chance they got. The two women argued that the next amendment should give everyone the right to vote. But if it wasn't going to include everyone, they said white women should come before Black men. Many of their arguments were racist. They used words like "ignorant" to describe Black men and words like "intelligent and capable" to describe white women.

It might surprise you that someone who started out fighting for justice would talk like that. Elizabeth Cady Stanton had supported voting rights for Black men in New York when she lived there. But now she felt that women's rights were being put on hold yet again. She was tired of waiting, and she resorted to racist arguments to make her point.

SUFFRAGIST AND RACIST

Sometimes it makes people uncomfortable when we talk about racism in historical figures. But the truth is, many people portrayed as heroes in history books held racist views. Susan B. Anthony is a great example of this. She argued publicly, over and over again, that white women should get the right to vote first because they were more intelligent and moral than Black men.

Some modern people have pointed to Susan B. Anthony's friendship with Frederick Douglass as proof that she wasn't racist. How could she have been if they were such good pals? It's true that Anthony and Douglass were friends. And it's also true that Anthony's views were racist. It was—and still is—possible for white people to be friends with Black people and still hold racist views.

Frederick Douglass spoke about his disappointment in Susan B. Anthony when she fought against Black men getting the right to vote, but he never stopped supporting woman suffrage.

Things got even worse in 1867. That year, the white men who could vote in Kansas were being asked to decide on two separate issues—suffrage for women and suffrage for Black men. Even though neither Stanton nor Anthony had ever lived in Kansas, both jumped into the discussion. They argued that white women should come first. They teamed up with a man named George Francis Train, a Northern white supremacist who had sympathized with the South during the Civil War.

Susan B. Anthony gave talks with Train. She stood beside him onstage as he said terribly racist things intended to make white voters afraid of Black men. Train promised that if Black men were given the right to vote, they'd see a case of a white woman being attacked by a Black man and then a trial "with twelve negro jurymen."

After all those speeches and all that arguing, white Kansas men voted no on both issues. So neither Black men nor women got the right to vote then.

You might think that would make Stanton and Anthony think twice about having such a cozy relationship with a man like George Train, but it didn't. They announced a new speaking tour with him. Train also gave them money to start a newspaper called the *Revolution*. Its goals were to gain voting rights for women and to defeat the Fifteenth Amendment.

Susan B. Anthony defended her decision in the new paper.

SO LONG AS MR. TRAIN SPEAKS NOBLY FOR THE WOMAN, WHY SHOULD WE REPUDIATE HIS SERVICES?

In other words: As long as he's on our side, why would we push him away?

Anthony said it didn't matter to her that Train used the most offensive words to describe Black people. All that mattered was that he supported her goals.

Stanton agreed in a letter she wrote to her friend Olympia Brown.

If the Devil himself had come up and said ladies I will help you establish a paper I should have said Amen!

Stanton also made racist and anti-immigrant remarks in some of her talks. She reminded white women that the Fifteenth Amendment would give the right to vote to not only Black men but immigrants, too. She used offensive stereotypical names for Irish, African American, German, and Chinese men in an 1869 speech.

THINK OF PATRICK AND SAMBO AND HANS AND YUNG TANG, WHO DO NOT KNOW THE DIFFERENCE BETWEEN A MONARCHY AND A REPUBLIC, WHO CANNOT READ THE DECLARATION OF INDEPENDENCE OR WEBSTER'S SPELLING BOOK, MAKING LAWS FOR LYDIA MARIA CHILDS, LUCRETIA MOTT, OR FANNY KEMBLE.

Those women she mentioned were notable suffrage leaders, and Stanton's feelings were clear. If anyone deserved the right to vote, it was educated white women like her.

Sometimes, modern people look at these racist views and make excuses for their historical heroines. Wasn't that just the way people thought back then? In this case, the answer is no. Even at the time, many people in the movement were horrified by Stanton's and Anthony's words. Lucy Stone begged them to stop giving such divisive talks.

Tensions over the Fifteenth Amendment came to a head at an AERA meeting in May 1869.

... THEN THEY WILL HAVE AN URGENCY TO OBTAIN THE BALLOT EQUAL TO OUR OWN.

VOTES

BUT SUSAN B. ANTHONY WASN'T MOVED. SHE INTRODUCED A RESOLUTION ASKING THE GROUP TO SUPPORT "EDUCATED SUFFRAGE."

SHE ASKED EVERYONE TO ACTIVELY FIGHT AGAINST THE FIFTEENTH AMENDMENT.

LUCY STONE STOOD UP AND URGED ANTHONY TO WITHDRAW THAT REQUEST.

I THANK GOD FOR THE FIFTEENTH AMENDMENT, AND HOPE THAT IT WILL BE ADOPTED IN EVERY STATE. I WILL BE THANKFUL IN MY SOUL IF ANY BODY CAN GET OUT OF THE TERRIBLE PIT.

Most people at that meeting agreed with Lucy Stone. Anthony's motion failed. But so did Stone's attempt to bring people together.

Elizabeth Cady Stanton and Susan B. Anthony refused to stay in a group that supported Black men getting the vote before white women. They left the AERA and formed a new group they called the National Woman Suffrage Association, or NWSA. Its members supported a woman suffrage amendment but also spent much of their time fighting the Fifteenth Amendment. If women couldn't have the right to vote, they argued, Black men shouldn't have it, either.

Meanwhile, Lucy Stone and her allies took what was left of the AERA and formed a new group, the American Woman Suffrage Association, or AWSA. Stone made it her group's mission to campaign for universal suffrage—the right for *everyone* to vote. The AWSA supported the Fifteenth Amendment and pushed for a woman suffrage amendment to be next. Lucy Stone and her husband, Henry Blackwell, started their own publication, called the *Woman's Journal,* to help promote those ideas.

The AWSA also decided to focus its efforts on state laws. For now, it was still up to individual states to decide whether women had the right to vote. Maybe if enough states changed their laws, it would help bring support for the amendment, too.

FOUR
TWO STEPS FORWARD, ONE STEP BACK

Despite the efforts of some white suffragists, the Fifteenth Amendment was ratified in 1870. Black men had finally won the right to vote! By then, state-by-state efforts to win woman suffrage were starting to pay off, too.

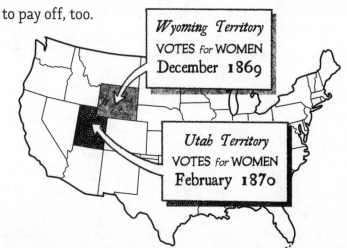

Wyoming Territory
VOTES for WOMEN
December 1869

Utah Territory
VOTES for WOMEN
February 1870

Around that time, some women were taking a closer look at the wording of the Fourteenth Amendment. Even though it included that line about "male citizens," the first part said only that states couldn't deny "citizens" their rights. Maybe if women tested the law by *trying* to vote, a court would decide that they were citizens after all and couldn't be denied that right. It was worth a try, wasn't it?

Lucy Stone was one of about 170 women who tested the law in New Jersey in 1868. When the women showed up to vote, they were simply turned away. The Grimké sisters led another group of women to try to vote in Massachusetts. And in Washington, DC, Mary Ann Cary registered, too, but wasn't allowed to vote.

In 1872, Susan B. Anthony and fifteen other women went to a Rochester barbershop that had been designated as a voter registration site and announced that they'd come to register to vote. They said they had every right, under the Fourteenth Amendment. The men in charge that day had no clue how to handle the situation, so they just let the women register.

On Election Day, those women showed up to vote. No one tried to stop them. They voted and went home.

But a few weeks later, an officer showed up at Susan B. Anthony's house to arrest her. Women weren't allowed to vote, he explained, so by voting, she'd broken the law. Anthony made the officer wait while she went to change her dress. Then she demanded that he put her in handcuffs. If he wanted to arrest her for voting, he was going to have to do it right.

When Susan B. Anthony went to court, she pleaded not guilty. Before her trial, she spent three weeks touring the county, giving speeches about what happened to her. She argued she never should have been arrested.

> CLEARLY, THEN, THERE IS NO CONSTITUTIONAL GROUND FOR THE EXCLUSION OF WOMEN FROM THE BALLOT-BOX IN THE STATE OF NEW YORK.
>
> NO BARRIERS, WHATEVER, STAND TO-DAY BETWEEN WOMEN AND THE EXERCISE OF THEIR RIGHT TO VOTE, SAVE THOSE OF PRECEDENT AND PREJUDICE.

The prosecutor complained about her speeches. How was he supposed to get a fair trial when Miss Anthony was so popular? He moved the trial to another county, but Susan B. Anthony went and gave speeches there, too.

When her trial began on June 17, 1873, the jury was made up of twelve men. Just men. Back then women weren't allowed to be on juries, either. The prosecutor made his case, and then Anthony's lawyer stepped up to speak. He said the only reason Susan B. Anthony was being charged with a crime was because she was a woman.

IF THE SAME ACT HAD BEEN DONE BY HER BROTHER UNDER THE SAME CIRCUMSTANCES,

THE ACT WOULD HAVE BEEN NOT ONLY INNOCENT BUT HONORABLE AND LAUDABLE;

BUT HAVING BEEN DONE BY A WOMAN, IT WAS SAID TO BE A CRIME.

So what did Susan B. Anthony say when it was her turn to speak in court and defend herself? Nothing. Because she didn't get a turn. The judge ordered the jurors to find her guilty, and they did. The next day, the judge sentenced her to a one-hundred-dollar fine, and then Anthony finally got to talk. She said no way would she even pay a dollar of his unfair fine.

You might guess that the judge threw Susan B. Anthony in jail then, but he didn't. He let her go. That meant she couldn't appeal the decision. Her goal had been to vote as a test of the law, to find out if a court would decide that the Fourteenth Amendment protected women's rights, too. But her case never made it to a higher court.

Later on, Virginia Minor, a woman who was arrested for voting in Missouri, took her case all the way to the

US Supreme Court, the highest court in the land. The justices ruled against her. They said the Fourteenth Amendment did *not* give women the right to vote. The issue was still up to the states.

NOPE.

Suffragists went back to work, trying to convince states to approve votes for women. They pushed for a national amendment, too. One was finally introduced in Congress in 1878. But it wouldn't be voted on for another nine years, and then it didn't pass.

Every year, suffragists went to Washington, DC, to lobby for the amendment. Every year, they were told the same thing: Woman suffrage was a state issue. They'd have to go back to the states to get support.

Eventually, Susan B. Anthony and Lucy Stone started wondering if they'd be better off working together again. They finally made up after their fierce battle over the Fifteenth Amendment. In 1890, they merged the two groups they were running into one, the National American Woman Suffrage Association, or NAWSA. Elizabeth Cady Stanton was its first president, but Susan B. Anthony took over the job in 1892.

AERA + NWSA = NAWSA

By then, there were new voices in the suffrage movement. One was Carrie Chapman Catt, a young teacher who was great at planning and getting people organized for meetings and letter-writing campaigns. By the 1890s, she and other women had convinced a few states to give women the right to vote. But not all women supported their efforts.

That may seem hard to understand. Why would anyone argue against their own right to vote? But in those days, the idea of women being involved in politics was new and scary to people. Some women argued that voting would weaken their role as mothers. They were busy *raising* voters and future leaders. Did they really have time to *be* voters, too?

Besides, anti-suffragists argued, women were already represented in government—by the men in their lives who could vote. And if they happened to disagree with the votes those men cast . . . well . . . they shouldn't. Anti-suffragists held their own protest in 1886.

IT IS OUR FATHERS, BROTHERS, HUSBANDS, AND SONS WHO REPRESENT US AT THE BALLOT-BOX. OUR FATHERS AND OUR BROTHERS LOVE US; OUR HUSBANDS ARE OUR CHOICE AND ONE WITH US; OUR SONS ARE WHAT WE MAKE THEM. WE DO THEREFORE RESPECTFULLY PROTEST AGAINST ANY LEGISLATION TO ESTABLISH "WOMAN SUFFRAGE" IN OUR LAND OR IN ANY PART OF IT.

—NATIONAL ASSOCIATION OPPOSED TO WOMAN SUFFRAGE

Just like the well-off white women fighting for suffrage, most of the women fighting against it had plenty of power already, thanks to their wealthy husbands. They weren't the people who most needed changes in the laws in order to survive.

But the funny thing is, to make their point about how bad suffrage would be, those women had to go out and give talks. They had to step out of their usual roles as ladies. They had to break some of those old rules they were trying to protect. So in a way, they helped show that things were changing in America, no matter what.

But the progress was terribly slow. It was clear to many early suffrage leaders that they might not see success in their lifetimes. So they passed the battle on to their daughters.

Alice Stone Blackwell was the daughter of Lucy Stone and Henry Blackwell. She was shy when she was little but overcame it to join the movement. She worked at her parents' newspaper, the *Woman's Journal*. When Lucy died in 1893, her last words were to Alice: "Make the world better."

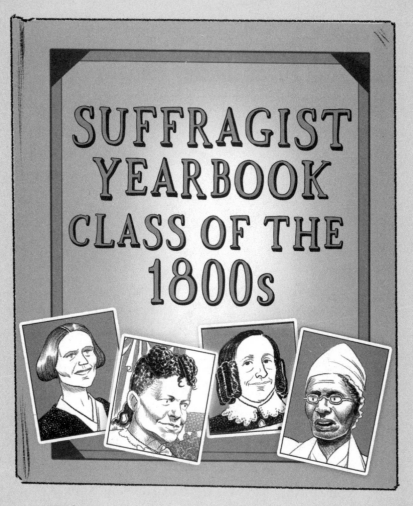

SUFFRAGIST
YEARBOOK
CLASS OF THE
1800s

We hear a lot about Elizabeth Cady Stanton's and Susan B. Anthony's work for woman suffrage in the 1800s, but many other women made important contributions, too.

Most Likely to Bet the Farm on Her Beliefs

ABBY KELLEY FOSTER was an abolitionist and suffragist. She and her husband started a network of antislavery newspapers. Abby Kelley Foster was giving speeches about women's rights long before the Seneca Falls convention. Women weren't allowed to speak in churches back then, so she gave her talks in apple orchards instead. She trained Lucy Stone and Susan B. Anthony to be activists. In 1870, Abby and her husband refused to pay their taxes because she couldn't vote. They said it was "taxation without representation," being forced to pay taxes without the right to vote. This happened three times. Each time, the government took their farm away and auctioned it off. And each time, the Fosters' friends bought it and gave it back to them.

The Keeping-What's-Hers Award

ERNESTINE ROSE was another antislavery woman who spoke up for her right to give talks. Rose was an immigrant who had come to New York in 1836. She thought that the state's law about married women not being able to keep their own property was the dumbest thing ever. So she led a push to get the law changed. In 1848, New York passed the Married Women's Property Act, which said that women who owned property when they were single could keep it after they got married.

Most Likely to Never Give Up

NAOMI TALBERT ANDERSON spoke at a suffrage convention in Chicago in 1869. She lectured throughout the Midwest and didn't give up her work even after her husband died. She learned hairdressing so she'd be able to support her children, and she kept on speaking and writing about women's rights and fighting racial prejudice.

The Power-Couple Award

LUCY STONE was the first woman from Massachusetts to earn a college degree. She was independent and kept her own last name when she married **HENRY BLACKWELL**. The couple fought for abolition as well as women's rights. Stone gave antislavery talks all around the Northeast, ignoring people who said it was an "unwomanly" thing to do. She and Blackwell started their own newspaper to fight for voting rights.

Most Likely to Be Misquoted

SOJOURNER TRUTH, a woman who had once been enslaved, gave a talk at a women's rights convention in Ohio in 1851. She spoke about how women were equal to men in many ways. Her now-famous talk is known as the "Ain't I a Woman" speech, but it turns out that might be based on bad information. There are actually two versions of Truth's speech. "Ain't I a Woman" comes from the version that was published in a famous history of the suffrage movement. In that book, from the late 1800s, Truth's talk is written in dialect that makes her sound less educated than she really was. But a newspaper report from the time of the actual convention isn't like that.

I HAVE AS MUCH MUSCLE AS ANY MAN, AND CAN DO AS MUCH WORK AS ANY MAN. . . . I HAVE PLOWED AND REAPED AND HUSKED AND CHOPPED AND MOWED, AND CAN ANY MAN DO MORE THAN THAT? I HAVE HEARD MUCH ABOUT THE SEXES BEING EQUAL; I CAN CARRY AS MUCH AS ANY MAN, AND CAN EAT AS MUCH, TOO, IF I CAN GET IT.

Truth was often portrayed as a stereotypical enslaved woman from the South. But really, she was from New York and had grown up speaking Dutch. Despite having been misrepresented, she is remembered as an important leader in the fight for women's rights.

Most Likely to Be Courageous in the Face of Hate

HARRIET FORTEN PURVIS was born into a free Black family in Philadelphia in 1810. Her father, who was a sailmaker, refused to work on any ships that might be involved in the slave trade. When he learned that his children couldn't go to Philadelphia's fancy private schools because they were Black, he worked with a woman named Grace Bustill Douglass to set up their own school. It offered Black kids the same high level of education.

Harriet grew up to be an activist, too. In 1838, she attended a Philadelphia antislavery convention with her husband, who had lighter

skin. People mistook them for an interracial couple and formed a mob after they saw him helping her from their carriage. Harriet Forten Purvis never backed down. Later she and her sister organized the Fifth National Women's Rights Convention in Philadelphia. Harriet's daughter Hattie would become that group's first African American vice president.

Suffragists in Training

CARRIE CHAPMAN grew up on a farm in Iowa, and she loved animals. She'd bring insects and reptiles into the house to observe them. When they died, she'd pickle them in her mom's jam jars. According to family legend, Carrie showed up with some rattlesnake eggs one day and tucked them behind the stove . . . where they started hatching! Her dad tossed them in the fire and put an end to that experiment.

When Carrie was thirteen, her father and older brother were on their way out to vote in the election of 1872. But Carrie noticed that her mom wasn't getting ready to go out. When she asked why her mother wasn't going to vote, the men laughed. So did her mom. When her dad explained that women couldn't vote, Carrie was angry. Her mother knew just as much about politics as her father did—maybe even more—so why shouldn't she be able to vote?

ANNA HOWARD SHAW was born in England but moved to the Michigan frontier as a child. She wanted to be a preacher and practiced giving talks to the trees in the forest. All that practice came in handy. She ended up becoming the Methodist Protestant Church's first female minister, as well as an advocate for woman suffrage.

FIVE
NEW CENTURY, NEW IDEAS

By 1900, the struggle for woman suffrage was in a bit of a rut. Women could vote in Wyoming, Colorado, Utah, and Idaho, but four years had passed without any more states getting on board. The national amendment was being ignored, too. But a new group of leaders brought new energy to the movement. And across the sea, British women fighting for equality inspired some exciting ideas about how to do battle.

Carrie Chapman Catt, that farm girl who loved animals, had grown up by then. She took over NAWSA when Susan B. Anthony retired in 1900. Unfortunately, Catt sometimes carried on Anthony's legacy of racism. In the late 1800s, Catt gave numerous speeches that argued against voting rights for new immigrants.

EVERY YEAR, WE ARE RECEIVING FEWER GOOD PEOPLE AND MORE OF THE SLUM ELEMENT.

Catt told people that new immigrants from southern and eastern Europe weren't as intelligent or patriotic as the old ones who came from Germany and England, as *her* ancestors had. She said these new immigrants were making a mess of everything. The only solution was giving white women the right to vote. Then they'd outnumber all those immigrants and make better decisions.

Catt also gave a speech called "Subject and Sovereign," in which she argued against Native American men getting the right to vote. She said by giving voting rights to Sioux men in the West, the government was creating new sovereigns, or rulers, that white women would have to follow.

When Catt took over NAWSA, she really wanted support from women in the South. Many white Southern women liked the idea of women voting, as long as that didn't include Black women. So in 1903, NAWSA prepared a statement suggesting that states should be able to develop their own positions on suffrage. In other words, it gave the South permission to discriminate against Black women.

As you can imagine, Black women who had been working for suffrage all along were upset. They weren't surprised, though. For the most part, the white women running the suffrage movement had left Black women out of the conversation. Their only option was to form their own groups.

Black women in the United States had already been working for their communities for a long time. Women like Mary Church Terrell, Mary McLeod Bethune, and Josephine St. Pierre Ruffin pushed for equality on their own terms. They created welfare groups to help people. They founded schools and health centers and orphanages.

Now they turned their attention to the battle for woman suffrage. They figured they needed the right to vote as much as anyone. Being Black *and* women meant that they faced twice as much discrimination. Sojourner Truth, Harriet Forten Purvis, Adella Hunt Logan, and Mary Church Terrell all spoke out about this "double burden."

Mary Church Terrell

> *Not only are colored women with ambition and aspiration handicapped on account of their sex, but they are everywhere baffled and mocked on account of their race. . . . Not only because they are women, but because they are colored women, are discouragement and disappointment meeting them at every turn.*

—MARY CHURCH TERRELL

Mary Church Terrell was born into a family of people who had been enslaved. She became one of the first Black women in the United States to earn a college degree. Later, she taught college and became involved in education issues.

In 1892, one of Terrell's friends was lynched. She was so angry that she had to act. Terrell joined forces with journalist Ida B. Wells to speak out against lynchings. She also became friends with Frederick Douglass and Susan B. Anthony and attended suffrage meetings.

The ongoing violence against Black people was one of the issues that led Terrell and others to form clubs for Black women's civic and political engagement. Like white women's organizations, these clubs took on health, education, and suffrage issues. They focused on fighting racism and building the resources of the Black community. Terrell's motto was "lifting as we climb." In other words, she believed that Black women who made progress would bring others along with them. In 1896, she was one of the founders and first president of the National Association of Colored Women (NACW), a coalition of Black women's groups.

Ida B. Wells was also instrumental in raising awareness of Black women's issues. Born into enslavement, she wasn't even five feet tall, but she made a big mark on the world as a journalist, suffragist, and civil rights leader.

Her work is believed to have started with an 1884 train ride in Tennessee. She'd bought a first-class ticket and was seated in the ladies' car but was asked to move to another car. Wells said no, and when three white men tried to remove her, she fought back. Afterward, she sued the railroad and

won. But Tennessee's Supreme Court later overturned that decision.

Ida B. Wells also led a major campaign against lynching. She made it her mission to name the many victims of violent racism who might otherwise have been forgotten. As a writer, she told stories of African American life that had often been ignored.

In 1895, she got married and became Ida B. Wells-Barnett. That same year, she published a history of lynching in America.

Wells-Barnett was a powerful speaker. She traveled across the country and overseas to raise awareness of lynching and racism in the United States. Her work eventually led to the passing of several anti-lynching laws.

She was a force in the woman suffrage movement, too. But like other Black women, Wells-Barnett found that white women's groups weren't very welcoming. Wells-Barnett often criticized even her friends and allies when she felt they weren't fully committed to the cause.

"She didn't suffer fools, and she saw fools everywhere," her grandson was quoted as saying in her obituary.

In 1913, Wells-Barnett founded the Alpha Suffrage Club, the first Black woman suffrage club in Chicago. The group became a well-known political force and urged Black women to vote as a group to help win elections.

Bostonian Josephine St. Pierre Ruffin was an activist who had known the sting of racism since she was a girl. She had light skin, so many people assumed she was white. When school officials found out she had a Black parent, they kicked her out.

Ruffin became involved in civil rights and suffrage causes during the Civil War. From 1890 to 1897, she published the first newspaper by and for Black women, the *Woman's Era*. She also integrated the New England Women's Club, changing the rules so that both white and Black women could be members.

Ruffin worked with Julia Ward Howe and Lucy Stone to form the American Woman Suffrage Association, or AWSA. Ruffin fought for voting rights alongside many white women, but when she saw racism, her newspaper wasn't afraid to call it out.

> *The exclusion of colored women and girls from nearly all places of respectable employment is due mostly to the meanness of American (white) women.*

Ruffin also founded the Woman's Era Club, a group dedicated to anti-lynching and other antiracism efforts as well as woman suffrage. It was the first Black women's club in Boston and the second in the country. But you didn't have to be Black to be in the club; some white women were early members, too.

Black women's clubs across the country supported the anti-lynching work of Ida B. Wells-Barnett. But many white women who fought for voting rights still approved of the lynching of Black men. One of those white women was Rebecca Ann Latimer Felton, who became the first woman to serve in the US Senate. She used terrible slurs in talking about Black men. She even argued that those illegal lynchings were necessary to protect white women.

The racist views of some white suffragists were one reason Black women decided to form their own groups. In 1895, Ruffin brought Black women's clubs together for the First National Conference of the Colored Woman in America. Notable women including Wells and Harriet Tubman were there. Eventually, as the women realized they were all working toward the same goals, many groups joined forces. The National Association of Colored Women grew out of those partnerships, and Mary Church Terrell was its first president. Ruffin served as her vice president.

Adella Hunt Logan wrote nationally published articles and organized suffrage efforts among Black women in Alabama. Logan argued that Black women had to organize themselves because it was pretty clear that white women weren't going to include them. Logan often passed as a white woman because of her light skin, so she was able to go to meetings of white suffragists and bring back news to her own community.

Nannie Helen Burroughs promoted suffrage via the National Baptist Convention's Women's Auxiliary.

Burroughs (left) holds a banner for the Banner State Woman's National Baptist Convention.

She argued that getting the vote would help defeat white supremacists in the South and improve conditions for Black people. She also opened a training school in Washington, DC, to help Black women get jobs to support themselves.

Mary McLeod Bethune was the youngest of seventeen children born to enslaved parents. After the Civil War, she attended segregated South Carolina schools and went on to build her own schools in Black communities. In 1904, she created the Daytona Literary and Industrial Training  School for Negro Girls and later merged it with an all-male school to form Bethune-Cookman College in Daytona Beach, Florida. Bethune served as president, one of the few women of any race to serve as a college president.

In the 1900s, Bethune turned her attention to the suffrage movement. But like many Black women, she found that she wasn't welcome in the white women's groups. Instead, she joined the Equal Suffrage League, which grew out of the National Association of Colored

Women. She continued to work for voting rights throughout her life.

Later, Bethune would become an adviser to President Franklin D. Roosevelt. She served as director of Negro Affairs in the National Youth Administration and was also assistant director of the Women's Army Corps and special assistant to the secretary of war. During that time, she worked on the development of the United Nations, an organization made up of countries from around the world coming together to solve problems and promote peace.

Meanwhile, some white suffrage leaders were changing roles. There wasn't much progress happening with that national amendment, so Carrie Chapman Catt decided to focus more of her efforts on voting rights in the states. In 1904, she stepped down as president of NAWSA, and Anna Howard Shaw took over the job. Like Susan B. Anthony and Carrie Chapman Catt, Shaw was a gifted speaker. And just like Anthony and Catt, she sometimes said racist things when she was talking to people in the South.

At a 1903 meeting in New Orleans, Shaw was asked a question about voting rights for Black people. She made it clear that she thought white women's rights should come first.

YOU HAVE PUT THE BALLOT IN THE HANDS OF YOUR BLACK MEN, THUS MAKING THEM THE POLITICAL SUPERIORS OF WHITE WOMEN. NEVER BEFORE IN THE HISTORY OF THE WORLD HAVE MEN MADE FORMER SLAVES THE POLITICAL MASTERS OF THEIR FORMER MISTRESSES!

Racism wasn't the only thing dividing the suffragists. Some young women thought NAWSA's leaders were too quiet, too polite, and too patient. *Years* were passing with no real progress. Why weren't things happening faster? Maybe it was time to stop being so proper and ladylike all the time. And maybe it was time to include more voices.

One of Elizabeth Cady Stanton's kids, Harriot Stanton Blatch, grew up to join the suffrage movement. She agreed with Elizabeth Cady Stanton that women should have the right to vote. But she *really* disagreed with some of her mom's other ideas. When Elizabeth Cady Stanton was giving talks in favor of "educated suffrage" that left out Black women and working-class immigrants, Blatch challenged her mom publicly with a written piece in the *Woman's Journal*. Blatch argued that working-class women had way more knowledge than wealthy women had about the issues that affected them, like housing for the poor. She said working-class women needed the vote to improve their conditions.

In 1907, Blatch founded a group called the Equality League of Self-Supporting Women for women who worked outside the home. Two hundred women showed up for the first meeting and demanded the right to vote. The women held all sorts of jobs; there were doctors and lawyers as well as shirtmakers, book-binders, and cap makers. A month later, some of those women spoke in front of New York's lawmakers—the first working-class women to do so.

Blatch's group organized parades and open-air meetings, too. Until then, most suffrage leaders had been fairly well-off—women who could afford to rent big halls for meetings or publish newspapers. But anyone could have a meeting on the street. And that encouraged more working-class women to speak up for their rights.

IMMIGRANTS—
THEY GET THE JOB DONE

Many of the women who worked in New York City's factories were recent arrivals to America. Rose Schneiderman was a Jewish immigrant who had come from Russian Poland and started working on the Lower

East Side at the age of thirteen. She was sixteen years old and working at a cap factory when she began organizing other women to fight for their right to vote—and to have better working conditions.

Schneiderman worked with Harriot Stanton Blatch and the Equality League of Self-Supporting Women, drumming up support for working women's rights. She was a well-

known speaker who traveled to different states giving talks on woman suffrage. Later, in the 1930s, Schneiderman helped change New York State's laws to establish a minimum wage and an eight-hour workday.

Much of the inspiration for these bold new ways of speaking up came from across the Atlantic Ocean, where British women were fighting an equal-rights battle of their own. Theirs was a lot louder.

In 1903, a British woman named Emmeline Pankhurst had started a group called the Women's Social and Political Union, or WSPU. It had a bold motto:

DEEDS NOT WORDS

For years, women had been politely asking for equal rights and getting nowhere. Pankhurst believed it was time for drastic changes to how they were asking.

BY 1906, BRITISH WOMEN WERE HOLDING DEMONSTRATIONS, SHOUTING DOWN GOVERNMENT SPEAKERS, AND EVEN BREAKING THE LAW TO GET ATTENTION FOR THEIR CAUSE.

SOME THREW STONES THROUGH OFFICE WINDOWS . . .

. . . OR SET FIRES IN MAILBOXES.

THEY CUT TELEPHONE WIRES, VANDALIZED TRAIN CARS, AND EVEN BURNED DOWN SOME BUILDINGS.

THEY GOT ARRESTED AND THROWN IN JAIL,

WHERE MANY WERE BEATEN BY MALE GUARDS.

WHEN THE WOMEN HAD HUNGER STRIKES TO PROTEST HOW THEY WERE BEING TREATED, THEY WERE FORCE-FED, WITH TUBES SHOVED DOWN THEIR THROATS OR NOSES.

WHILE ALL THIS WAS HAPPENING, AMERICAN SUFFRAGISTS WERE WATCHING —

AND LEARNING.

One of those American suffragists was Alice Paul, a social
worker from New Jersey who was
studying in Britain and joined
the protests. Paul was arrested
and thrown in jail at least half a
dozen times. That was how she
met her friend Lucy Burns. Both
women were arrested during a
London protest in 1909.

When the two friends returned to America, the
women's rights movement felt quiet and boring com-
pared to the battle they'd left behind in Britain. And

there was still no progress on that national amendment.

Paul and Burns thought it was time to try something new. In 1912, they went to NAWSA and asked if they could take over the group's Congressional Committee. It had been set up to push for the national amendment, but since the amendment wasn't going anywhere, the committee had all but given up.

Paul and Burns intended to change that. Their first step was planning a parade. But not just any parade. This parade would be impossible for America's leaders to ignore.

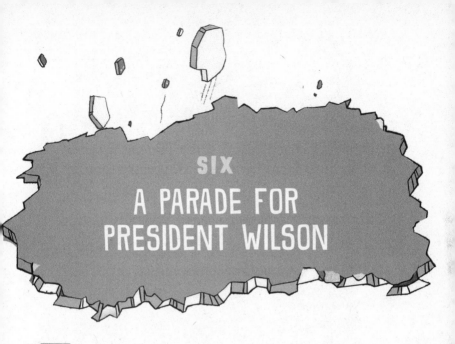

SIX

A PARADE FOR PRESIDENT WILSON

The idea was bold. Thousands of women from all over America would make their way to Washington, DC. They'd march in a huge parade on the day before Woodrow Wilson's inauguration. They would take their fight for equal rights straight to the nation's new president.

Alice Paul spent eight weeks planning the parade, and she had a lot of help.

New York City activist Rosalie Gardiner Jones organized a group of women to walk all the way from New York to Washington, DC, to get attention for the event.

Rosalie Gardiner Jones

That might sound like a fun idea, but keep in mind that it was the middle of winter! The women set out in February with a plan to walk nearly three hundred miles in sixteen days. The long march began with just sixteen women, wearing long brown wool capes. They passed out leaflets and gave speeches along the way. More women joined them at each town they passed.

Their long walk through the wind and snow did its job; it got attention. People talked about the women. Newspapers wrote stories about them. And despite the awful winter weather, the women arrived in time for the parade on March 3, 1913. It took hours to get everyone lined up.

Official Program
WOMAN SUFFRAGE
Procession

Washington D.C.
March 3, 1913

A young woman named Inez Milholland led the parade, dressed all in white and riding a horse named Gray Dawn that she'd borrowed from a friend.

Next came the amendment float, with a model of the Liberty Bell and a big banner demanding a woman suffrage amendment to the Constitution. The officers of NAWSA followed that float. Behind them came at least nine bands and twenty-six floats. Six golden chariots represented the first six states to give women the right to vote. And then came the women— thousands of them! They marched in groups representing their professions, states, and colleges. Some men and politicians marched, too.

The parade was a major accomplishment for woman suffrage leaders. But like the rest of the movement, the event was marked by racism. Some of the parade organizers worried that white women wouldn't want to march alongside Black women. They quietly discouraged Black women's groups from participating. Black women who wanted to attend were told they should march in their own group, in the back.

As you can imagine, Black women thought that was a pretty crummy invitation. Many decided to skip the parade and focus on their own work instead. But some marched anyway. Mary Church Terrell joined women from the newly formed African American

sorority Delta Sigma Theta at Howard University. They marched in their own group, separate from the white college women.

When Ida B. Wells-Barnett found out she was being told to march at the back of the parade, she was furious. No way was she going to do that!

Wells-Barnett stepped back as if she were going to march where she was told. But when the parade started, she jumped into the middle with the rest of her Illinois group, where she'd planned to march in the first place.

Up to eight thousand women marched, and around half a million people came out to watch. The parade started in front of the Capitol. At first everything went fine. For a while the streets were clear and the crowds were polite.

But soon the spectators—most of them white men—started harassing the women.

They shouted at the women, spit at them, and pinched them as they marched by. Some even tore off the women's badges and ripped their clothes. Then the men blocked the streets so the parade couldn't even continue.

Why were the men so angry? The women weren't breaking any laws. It was perfectly legal for them to march and share their ideas. The First Amendment to the Constitution guarantees people that right. But suddenly these men in the crowd were breaking the law to keep the women from exercising their rights.

The women's path grew narrow. The parade stalled for over an hour. All the while the crowd was growing louder and more dangerous.

You're probably wondering why no one arrested those men who were breaking the law. Why didn't somebody call the police?

The answer is because the police were already there. The women had a permit for the parade, so the city had officers on duty. Those officers were supposed to keep the peace and protect the women who were marching.

Instead, witnesses said, most of the officers just stood around and watched.

It was so bad that the United States Senate held a hearing later to figure out what had happened

I HAVE NEVER HEARD SUCH VULGAR, OBSCENE, SCURRILOUS, ABUSIVE LANGUAGE AS WAS HURLED AT US THAT DAY BY MEN . . . AND IT AMUSED THE POLICE.

Some people in the crowd tried to help the women who were being attacked. A group of college men tried to clear a path. Some Boy Scouts used their walking sticks to keep the spectators back. But the mob was huge. Federal troops had to be called in to get things under control. Finally, the women could finish their parade. They wrapped up with a rally at Continental Hall.

The energy of that day continued into Woodrow Wilson's presidency. The women led groups to visit Wilson at the White House. They brought petitions. They raised money and started a new weekly newspaper, the *Suffragist*. They kept pushing for that amendment to give women the right to vote.

A little over a month after the March parade, the women held another one to mark the opening session of Congress. It ended with an amendment being formally reintroduced on the Capitol steps—the same suffrage amendment from 1878. The women hoped this time, finally, their lawmakers would act on it.

MAKING ARGUMENTS WITH ART

Cartooning was an important part of the woman suffrage movement in the 1900s.

ROSE O'NEILL was a cartoonist who also created popular toys called Kewpie dolls. O'Neill got involved in the fight for voting rights with her comics.

Give Mother the Vote!

Our Food, Our Health
Our Play, Our Homes
Our Schools, Our Work

Are all regulated by Men's Votes. Think it over, and—

GIVE MOTHER THE VOTE!

An example of Rose O'Neill's Kewpie doll comics, supporting women's suffrage.

NINA ALLENDER was another talented suffragist-artist. She drew hundreds of cartoons for the *Suffragist*.

There was some progress after the 1913 parade in Washington, DC. Two more states—Montana and Nevada—gave women the right to vote. And *finally* the Senate voted on the woman suffrage amendment! It didn't pass, but at least that big parade got people talking.

Alice Paul and her friends wanted them to talk more! So they came up with even bolder ideas to get attention for the amendment. They started heckling President Wilson during speeches, interrupting to ask questions in the middle of his talks. That might not have been polite, but people noticed. They talked about the women's tactics and wrote about them in newspapers.

WHY WON'T YOU GIVE WOMEN THE RIGHT TO VOTE?!

You might think that the older women in NAWSA would be excited about getting attention for their cause. They'd been fighting for so long, and now those young activists were really shaking things up. Yay! Right?

Nope . . . not so much. The older women were uncomfortable with how loud Paul and her supporters had become. It felt impolite. Unladylike. They suggested to Alice Paul that she tone things down.

That didn't go over well. Paul didn't think the NAWSA women were being bold *enough*. She was tired of waiting for them to get things done.

Eventually, Alice Paul and Lucy Burns got thrown out of NAWSA. They kept working with their own group, the Congressional Union for Woman Suffrage, to try to get that amendment passed. Before long, they joined forces with another group out west, the Woman's Party, which believed in the same kinds of tactics.

When the Congressional Union and the Woman's Party merged, they called themselves the National Woman's Party. They made plans to shake things up even more—by taking their message straight to President Wilson.

That January, they started picketing the White House. The picketers showed up with banners every day, no matter the weather. It was their daily reminder to President Wilson that America's women still didn't have the right to vote.

For the first few months, White House guards were polite to the picketers. Sometimes they were even friendly. But the more the women questioned the president, the tenser things became.

It didn't help that just a few months after the pickets began, America went to war again. When the United States entered World War I, the quieter ladies of NAWSA took a break from lobbying for the amendment. They spent their time working for the war effort, just as they had during the Civil War.

But Alice Paul didn't believe in taking breaks. Her National Woman's Party kept picketing. Suffragists came from all over to help. Sometimes the picketers put Wilson's own words on their banners to show what a hypocrite he was, saying one thing but doing another. They pointed out that the president was fighting for freedom in Europe without supporting women's rights at home.

Some people were upset that the women wouldn't stop protesting during the war. That anger came to a head in June 1917, when the women picketed on a day Russian visitors were scheduled to visit the White

House. Angry people in the crowd grabbed the women's banner and tore it up. The women came back the next day with a new banner. Men in the crowd destroyed that one, too.

It's against the law to steal other people's things and destroy them. Surely this must be the part of the story where the police show up to arrest those men who stole the women's banners, right?

Wrong. The police issued a warning—but not to the violent men from the crowd. They warned the women! Officers even threatened to arrest them if they didn't stop picketing.

The women were bewildered. They had been picketing for six months. The laws in America hadn't changed. Citizens still had the right to peacefully protest. And the women weren't doing anything different. The only thing that had changed was that men in the crowd had started attacking them.

That warning didn't keep the picketers away. The next day they showed up with their banners, just like always—and got arrested. They were released, but a few days later more women were arrested. This time they were brought before a judge.

When the women refused to pay, the judge sent them to spend three days in the district jail.

Jail! Some people thought that would put an end to the picketing once and for all, but they obviously didn't know the suffragists very well. On Independence Day, the women were back in front of the White House with their banners. Again, men in the crowd attacked them. Again, the police arrested the women. And again, they were sentenced to three days in jail.

> **STOP BOTHERING THE PRESIDENT.**

Later that month, sixteen women, some of whom were grandmothers, were arrested and sent to a place called the Occoquan Workhouse in Virginia. It was known as a filthy prison where people were treated horribly.

This time the sentence wasn't three days. It was *sixty!*

People spoke up to complain about how unfair that was. The public outcry was so loud that President

Wilson was forced to set the women free after three days. Can you guess what they did when they left the workhouse?

They went right back to picketing. By mid-August, their banners were even more controversial. One referred to the president as "Kaiser Wilson," suggesting that Wilson had more sympathy for Germans who couldn't vote than he did for American women.

Men and boys tore the women's banners, their sashes, and even their clothes. They broke the banner poles and used them as weapons. When the women finally left, the mob followed them back to their headquarters and tried to storm the building. The women went inside and locked the door.

Lucy Burns showed up on the balcony, defiant, holding the National Woman's Party flag and the Kaiser banner. The crowd threw rotten eggs and fruit at her. They cheered for two men who climbed the

building and ripped the banners away. Someone fired gunshots at the building. The bullets just missed hitting two women inside.

The longer the women kept protesting, the harsher their punishments got. In October, police announced that anybody who picketed would be sentenced to six months in jail.

You can probably guess by now that Alice Paul still

didn't stop. In fact, she led a group of picketers the very next day.

It probably also doesn't surprise you to learn that the women were arrested. Paul and another suffragist, Rose Winslow, went on a hunger strike. They refused to eat as a way to protest their treatment.

The guards force-fed the women. They held each woman down, shoved a tube down her throat, and poured in a mixture of cold milk and raw eggs.

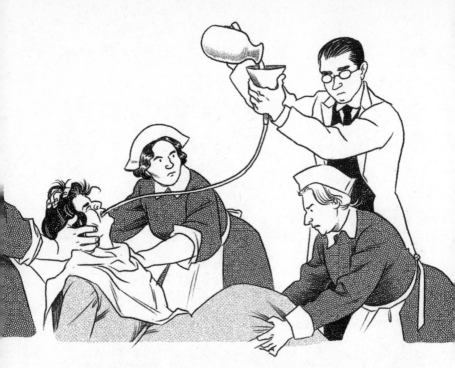

That went on every day for three weeks. Winslow snuck notes out of the jail so people would know what was happening. Supporters started gathering outside the workhouse to protest the women's treatment.

You might think that the women from NAWSA would be part of that crowd, offering support. But the truth is, the suffragists didn't always have one another's backs.

The NAWSA women had always thought it was a dumb idea to picket the White House, because they needed Wilson's support. In a letter to a fellow suffragist, NAWSA's president Anna Howard Shaw called the picketers "blank fools." She even seemed to hope harm would come to them.

J wish something would happen to Miss Paul and stop the whole business.

When something *did* happen—when Paul and the other women got attacked, arrested, thrown in jail, and beaten—NAWSA's leaders just sat by and watched.

On November 10, 1917, police arrested another forty-one women. Most of them ended up being sent to the workhouse. That night they were dragged down the hall and thrown into their cells so forcefully that some were injured. The guards wouldn't let them see a doctor. The women weren't even allowed to use the bathroom.

Lucy Burns was worried about her friends, so she tried to check on them by calling everyone's name. The warden ordered her to stop. When she didn't, he had her shackled to her cell

door with her hands chained over her head for the rest of the night.

That came to be known as the Night of Terror. The workhouse warden told one woman that his goal was to put an end to the protests, even if it cost the lives of some of the women, and he said it probably would.

Even after that awful night, the suffragists didn't give up. They staged another hunger strike, which led to more forced feedings. Rose Winslow smuggled a note out of jail to let people know what that was like.

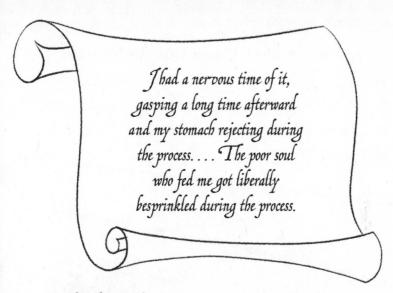

I had a nervous time of it, gasping a long time afterward and my stomach rejecting during the process. . . . The poor soul who fed me got liberally besprinkled during the process.

In other words: It was absolutely terrible to be force-fed. And the experience was pretty gross for the people doing the feeding, too. "Besprinkled" is just a nicer word for "puked on."

When news got out, the public was horrified. It became clear that the prison warden's plan was backfiring. The suffragists weren't being silenced at all. They were getting *more* attention and *more* support.

At the end of November, public sympathy for the women forced the government to simply let them go. By that time, the women were too weak and exhausted to stand. But their sacrifice had made a difference.

Finally, President Wilson changed his mind. In January 1918, he announced his support for a constitutional amendment giving women the right to vote. Now, with Wilson's support, the amendment felt like a real possibility.

SUFFRAGE SONGS

As the idea of woman suffrage became more popular, the movement found its way into popular music.

The 1917 White House pickets inspired a song that suffragists sang sometimes while they were protesting or sitting in jail. It was published in the *Suffragist* in November 1917, with a note that it should be sung to the tune of "The Ballad of Captain Kid," an old sailing song that goes like this:

My name is William Kidd, as I sailed, as I sailed
My name is William Kidd, as I sailed
My name is William Kidd, God's laws I did forbid
And most wickedly I did, as I sailed, as I sailed . . .

The suffragists' version was called "We Worried Woody Wood," a reference to President Woodrow Wilson.

We worried Woody-wood,
As we stood, as we stood,
We worried Woody-wood,
As we stood . . .

Other verses went on to talk about how women asked for the vote, were sent to jail, and received poor treatment there.

We asked them for some air,
As we choked, as we choked.
We asked them for some air,
As we choked.
We asked them for some air,
And they threw us in a lair,
They threw us in a lair, so we choked.

THE SUFFRAGISTS AT HOME

Some of the suffragists, like Ida B. Wells-Barnett, Elizabeth Cady Stanton, and Lucy Stone, were married and had children. But many others chose to remain single. Among them was Susan B. Anthony, who often complained that her fellow suffragists' kids got in the way of their mission. Sometimes she'd come over to help out with Elizabeth Cady Stanton's seven kids so her friend could get some work done. Once, while Anthony was babysitting, the older Stanton boys threw their younger brother into the water with corks attached to his body to see if he'd float. (He didn't, so it's a good thing she was there!)

Other suffragists never got married but had long-term loving relationships with other women. Women weren't allowed to marry other women back then—that wasn't even talked about—but some suffragists lived with their partners. Sometimes these relationships were called "Boston marriages." The term was inspired by an 1886 novel, *The Bostonians,* about a romantic relationship between two wealthy women in Boston.

NAWSA president Anna Howard Shaw and Lucy Anthony (Susan B. Anthony's niece) had a relationship like this. They lived together, traveled together, and worked together fighting for women's rights. Carrie Chapman Catt had been married, but after her husband George died, she lived with her female partner, Mollie Hay. When Catt died, she chose to be buried next to Mollie, not George. Susan B. Anthony also had close relationships with other women throughout her life, especially with fellow suffragist Anna Dickinson, with whom she exchanged many loving notes.

These women didn't talk about their private lives much except to other suffragists; they knew that many people wouldn't approve. But within the movement, they talked openly about their relationships and their decisions not to marry men. Some thought they got more work done that way. Elizabeth Cady Stanton wrote a poem about that for Susan B. Anthony's seventieth birthday.

Better than to be any man's wife,
She says: To "the cause" devote your life;
Because husbands may die, or run away.
But the suffrage movement is here to stay.

EIGHT
FIGHTING FOR AN AMENDMENT

When you think of a law changing, you probably think of a big, important vote happening somewhere. But it takes more than one vote to change the Constitution. To pass an amendment for woman suffrage, there had to be a whole bunch of votes, and they all had to go the right way.

Remember that process for amending the Constitution? For an amendment to be approved, it has to get a two-thirds majority vote in the House of Representatives *and* in the Senate. And then three-quarters of the states have to vote yes for it to be ratified, or approved.

For years, women fighting for the right to vote had been waiting for that process to begin. On January 10, 1918, a day after President Wilson announced his support for the woman suffrage amendment, a vote was scheduled in the House of Representatives. If it passed, it would be the Nineteenth Amendment. People had also started calling it the Susan B. Anthony Amendment to honor her. Anthony had died in 1906 without seeing the results of her work.

A FILE FULL OF SECRETS

In addition to holding protests, the National Woman's Party worked behind the scenes to persuade lawmakers to support a suffrage amendment. The NWP kept a big file of index cards with information on each lawmaker so that women who met with them would know all about them. There were 581 cards—one for each member of Congress. The cards included information about the representatives' views on suffrage and even details of their personal lives. Some members of Congress were reportedly a little worried about just how many secrets the NWP had written on those cards!

When it came time for that vote in the House of Representatives, suffragists lined up early to get seats. They wanted to see this historic vote for themselves. They knew it would be close. Lawmakers understood how important the vote was, too. They made every effort to show up that day.

REPRESENTATIVE HENRY BARNHART OF INDIANA HAD BEEN SICK BUT ARRIVED ON A STRETCHER SO HE COULD VOTE.

THETUS SIMS FROM TENNESSEE SLIPPED ON THE ICE AND BROKE HIS SHOULDER THAT MORNING BUT REFUSED TO GO TO THE HOSPITAL BECAUSE HE WAS AFRAID HE WOULDN'T BE BACK IN TIME FOR THE VOTE.

CONGRESSMAN FREDERICK HICKS OF NEW YORK HAD BEEN AT HOME WITH HIS WIFE, WHO WAS SICK AND DYING, BUT HE CAME BACK TO DC, TOO. HIS WIFE HAD INSISTED THAT HE LEAVE HER SO HE'D BE THERE FOR THE VOTE.

VOTE!

When Congress convened, Representative Jeannette Rankin, who'd been elected by Montana voters in 1916, opened the debate. Dozens of speakers had their say until finally, at about five o'clock that evening, it was time for the vote. The suffragists held their breath.

When the final vote was called, the amendment was approved! The gallery erupted in cheers.

AMENDMENT MATH

For a constitutional amendment to pass, two-thirds of the members of each house of Congress need to approve it. The suffragists watching that vote in the House of Representatives on January 10, 1918, knew exactly how many yeses they needed for a victory.

There were 410 representatives voting on the amendment that day. We can set up a math problem to figure out how many votes were needed to pass the amendment.

$$\frac{2}{3} = \frac{n}{410}$$

This is a simple algebra problem where the letter *n* represents the number we don't know. In order to solve the problem, we multiply 2 × 410 and then divide by 3.

$$\frac{2}{3} \times \frac{n}{410} \qquad 820 = 3n$$

$$820 \div 3 = 3n \div 3$$

$$273 = n \text{ (with a remainder of 3)}$$

On the morning of January 10, 1919, 274 members of the House of Representatives voted yes, so the Susan

B. Anthony Amendment ended up passing by a single vote. Hurray!

But really, it was more of a "hurray for now." The battle wasn't over. Right away it became clear that the Senate wasn't ready to support votes for women. Suffragist leaders had been keeping track of senators' views, and they were still ten votes short. The Senate scheduled a vote but then postponed it and left for summer vacation without voting.

Suffragists didn't take the summer off, though.

Members of the National Woman's Party protest at Lafayette Monument in Washington, DC, in August 1918.

They kept working. On August 6, 1918, members of the National Woman's Party marched to Lafayette Monument, near the White House. The courts had thrown out all of the women's earlier arrests and convictions. Judges had pointed out that in the United States, it's not against the law to protest. So you might think people would respect the women's rights this time around.

Nope. One by one, as the women stepped up to speak, police arrested them. When they were sentenced to a workhouse, their supporters organized protests. Once again, the women had to be released before their sentences were up.

When the Senate went back to work, a vote was scheduled for October 1. President Wilson specifically asked the senators to vote yes on the amendment, but his support wasn't enough.

MORE AMENDMENT MATH

On October 1, 1918, America had forty-eight states. (Alaska and Hawaii weren't states yet.)

Each state had two senators, so there would be ninety-six men voting on the Susan B. Anthony Amendment.

Remember, two-thirds of those senators would have to vote yes for the amendment to move forward. If we set up our simple algebra problem and do the math, we can figure out how many votes were needed.

$$\frac{2}{3} = \frac{n}{96}$$

$$\frac{2}{3} \diagdown \frac{n}{96} \qquad 192 = 3n$$

$$192 \div 3 = 3n \div 3$$

$$64 = n$$

Of the ninety-six US senators voting, sixty-four would have to vote yes for the amendment to pass.

But when the vote was called, just sixty-two senators voted yes. The suffragists came up two votes short.
So they went back to picketing. When World War I
ended in November, they stepped up their efforts and
planned a big protest for the anniversary of the Boston

Tea Party, one of the events that had led up to the Revolutionary War.

The Boston Tea Party had taken place on December 16, 1773, when colonists dumped more than three hundred chests of tea into Boston Harbor. They had been protesting taxation without representation—the fact that they had to pay taxes even though they didn't have representatives in the British Parliament. In 1918, the suffragists argued that they were in the same situation, since they had to follow the laws of a nation that didn't let them vote.

So on December 16, more than three hundred women marched to the White House. They planned to burn speeches and books written by Woodrow Wilson. Wilson had announced his support for the amendment, but the suffragists wanted him to do more. And they sure didn't think he should be overseas, giving talks about freedom and democracy, when half of America's population couldn't even vote.

Wilson wasn't there to see the protest, because he was in France. In a way, that helped make the suffragists' point. One of the women who dropped President Wilson's words into the flames was eighty-three-year-old Olympia Brown.

I HAVE FOUGHT FOR LIBERTY FOR SEVENTY YEARS AND I PROTEST THE PRESIDENT'S LEAVING OUR COUNTRY WITH THIS OLD FIGHT HERE UNWON.

The Senate scheduled another vote for February 10, 1919. And the National Woman's Party held another protest the day before. This time the women announced they'd burn a portrait of President Wilson.

Burn a portrait of the president! That was a shocking, bold plan. Police showed up, ready to stop the women from following through.

But instead of making a big scene with a huge portrait of the president, the women pulled out a small cartoon of Wilson. They burned it so fast there was no time for the police to stop them.

When officers realized what was happening, they rushed in and arrested the women. Twenty-six went to jail, and the next day the Senate once again failed to approve the amendment.

Now were the women ready to give up?

Nope. Instead, Lucy Burns and other suffragists who'd spent time in prison went on a speaking tour all around the country. They chartered a railroad car to take them from city to city and called it the "Prison Special." Thousands of people came to hear them speak.

Suffragist Lucy Branham gives a speech on the "Prison Special" tour.

Suffragists also showed up to protest when President Wilson was scheduled to speak at the opera house in New York City on March 4. When the picketers approached the building, police officers beat them back with clubs and destroyed their banners. Soldiers and sailors attacked the women, too. They knocked them down and stole their pocketbooks and watches. Some women were left unconscious and bleeding. But they didn't back down. One of the suffragists, Elsie Hill, climbed up to a balcony, where she burned one of Wilson's speeches and shouted at the crowd.

You might still think that the police would arrest those men who were assaulting women and stealing things. Or maybe by now you understand what the women understood—that the police at that time weren't there to protect them. The men in the violent crowd weren't arrested. But the women were.

If that makes you angry, you're not alone. Newspapers wrote about the violence the women had to face that day. Some service members apologized for their fellow soldiers and sailors. Both NAWSA and the NWA used the publicity to make a demand. They urged President Wilson to call a special session of Congress to address the suffrage amendment.

And he did! That special session was scheduled for May 19, 1919.

All through that winter and spring, suffragists had worked to gather support. They'd been speaking and protesting and visiting lawmakers in their offices. Some lawmakers who had opposed the amendment changed their minds. But was it enough? This time, *both* houses of Congress would have to vote yes.

You might be thinking, *Wait a minute! Didn't the House of Representatives already do that?* The answer is yes. They did. But the Senate held things up for so long that the old vote had expired, so the House had to vote again. And remember, it takes a two-thirds majority vote in both houses of Congress to pass a constitutional amendment.

AMENDMENT MATH

This time some lawmakers were absent, so 393 members of the House of Representatives would be voting. How many votes would it take for the amendment to pass? Let's do our algebra problem to find out. . . .

$$\frac{2}{3} = \frac{n}{393}$$

$$\frac{2}{3} \diagdown \frac{n}{393} \qquad 786 = 3n$$

$$786 \div 3 = 3n \div 3$$

$$262 = n$$

So this time 262 members of the House would have to vote yes. When the roll call happened, there were more than enough votes: 304 yes to 89 no. The amendment passed the House.

And what about the Senate? Ninety-five senators were voting that day.

$$\frac{2}{3} = \frac{n}{95}$$

$$\frac{2}{3} \diagdown \frac{n}{95} \qquad 190 = 3n$$

$$190 \div 3 = 3n \div 3$$

$$63.333 = n$$

So sixty-three senators would have to vote yes in order for the suffrage amendment to pass. When it came time for the vote, the women held their breath yet again. . . .

Final vote:

65 YES
30 NO

Finally! After all of that picketing and lobbying and traveling, both houses of Congress had voted in favor of the suffrage amendment.

Yay! Right?

Kind of. But really it was just another "yay . . . for now." Remember how complicated it is to ratify an amendment? Passing both houses of Congress was a huge step forward, but for women to win the vote, the amendment also needed support in three-quarters of the states. So the women went right back to work.

NINE
THE BATTLE FOR TENNESSEE

Then it was May 1920. Three generations of women had been fighting for voting rights for decades. They'd kept it up through two wars, raising their voices and even sacrificing their freedom sometimes to make their point. Now it all came down to the states.

In order for the Susan B. Anthony Amendment to pass, three-quarters of the states had to approve it. The suffragists understood right away that it would be a fight. They had already done the amendment math.

AMENDMENT MATH

In 1920, there were still forty-eight states. (Alaska and Hawaii didn't become states until 1959.) So how many of those would need to approve the amendment to get that three-fourths majority? The suffragists had it all figured out.

$$\frac{3}{4} = \frac{n}{48}$$

$$\frac{3}{4} \times \frac{n}{48} \quad 144 = 3n$$

$$144 \div 3 = 3n \div 3$$

$$36 = n$$

Thirty-six states. That's how many would have to say yes to pass the amendment.

The suffragists had work to do. And if they wanted women to vote in the November 1920 presidential election, they'd have to work fast. They sent telegrams to governors all around the nation. They went on speaking tours, trying to rally support for the amendment.

For a state to ratify the amendment, the state's legislature—the lawmaking branch of government— had to vote on it. People in each state elected lawmakers to represent them in the legislature. And each state legislature had two houses, just as the US Congress did. So it was a long, long process.

Some states ratified the amendment right away. Illinois, Wisconsin, and Michigan were the first to approve it, on June 10. Eight more states said yes before the month was over. By the end of 1919, twenty-two states had ratified it. Just fourteen more to go!

One by one, as states approved the amendment, the National Woman's Party added stars to the ratification flag its members had created. By May 1920, there were thirty-five stars on the flag. The suffragists needed one more vote. Just one more!

National Woman's Party members track
progress on their ratification flag.

But some states had voted no, so the suffragists
were running out of chances to get that final yes vote.
There were just five states left that hadn't voted yet,
and lawmakers in those states had already gone home
for the summer. In order to get another state vote done
by November, at least one of those states' governors
would have to call a special session of the legislature.
Would a governor be willing to do that? And if he did,

would the lawmakers vote yes? The suffragists took a look at the five states that still had to vote. . . .

They decided that Vermont, Connecticut, and Tennessee were their best bets. But when the women asked the governors of Connecticut and Vermont to call a special legislative session, the governors said no.

That left Tennessee. There, thanks to some pressure from President Wilson, the governor agreed to call the legislature back so the vote could happen. But there was no guarantee the amendment would pass. Everyone knew the vote would be close, so activists on both sides showed up in Tennessee that summer, ready for a showdown.

Carrie Chapman Catt spent two months there, holding meetings and giving interviews, trying to pick up votes for the amendment. But no matter how hard she worked in the sweltering heat, the votes seemed to be slipping away.

That's because the people who opposed suffrage were also working hard that summer. Powerful men who ran businesses were worried about how women might vote once they had that right, and those men poured into Tennessee, too.

The United States Brewers' Association represented companies that sold alcoholic beverages. Many women supported Prohibition, the law that made it illegal to sell alcohol in the United States at that time. So the Brewers' Association sure didn't want women voting.

The Manufacturers' Association represented factories. Its members knew that many women supported laws to protect workers. Those women wanted a minimum wage so workers would be paid fairly. They wanted laws to prevent child labor and unsafe working conditions. The Manufacturers' Association opposed all of that, so it was also against women voting. So was

the railroad industry, which was very involved in politics and worried that women voting would mean less power for them.

It wasn't just powerful businesses fighting the suffragists. Some regular people fought the amendment, too. A Tennessee teacher named Josephine Anderson Pearson was vacationing in the mountains when she got a telegram ordering her to Nashville right away to battle the suffragists who had shown up in town.

Form 1204

WESTERN UNION
TELEGRAM

NEWCOMB CARLTON, PRESIDENT   GEORGE W. E. ATKINS, FIRST VICE-PRESIDENT

MRS. CATT ARRIVED. EXTRA
CALLED SESSION IMMINENT
BY THE GOVERNOR. OUR FORCES
ARE BEING NOTIFIED TO RALLY
AT ONCE. SEND ORDERS—
AND COME IMMEDIATELY.

Pearson was part of a group called the Southern Women's League for the Rejection of the Susan B. Anthony Amendment. The group's name explained what its members wanted—for that vote in Tennessee's legislature to fail.

Pearson's group was actually fine with women voting . . . as long as "women" meant only white women. Pearson explained her racist ideas in a letter that was widely distributed. She made it clear that she didn't support the amendment because she didn't want Black women to vote and she didn't want racial equality. She argued that the amendment would mean an end to white supremacy in the South, and she thought that was a terrible idea.

Can you imagine someone using *that* as an argument against women voting? You might be wondering if this is when suffragist leaders like Carrie Chapman Catt finally spoke up against the racism in their movement. Sadly, they didn't. Instead, Catt and others argued that suffrage wouldn't hurt white supremacy at all. They pointed out that Southern states had laws in place so Black men couldn't vote. Why wouldn't those laws apply to Black women, too? Alice Paul had made the same promises to white women in the South the year before.

NEGRO MEN CANNOT VOTE IN SOUTH CAROLINA, AND THEREFORE NEGRO WOMEN COULD NOT IF WOMEN WERE TO VOTE IN THE NATION.

Privately, some white suffragists did try to defend Black women as voters. But publicly? They mostly stayed quiet, even though Black women had helped lead the fight that had brought the amendment this far.

The arguments raged all summer. The special session of Tennessee's legislature opened on August 9, and the ratification amendment was introduced the next day. There was fiery debate, even though everyone knew there were enough votes for the measure to pass in the senate. And it did pass—twenty-five yeses to four nos.

Yay, right?

Not yet. Don't forget that there are two houses in each state legislature. So while the Tennessee Senate had approved the amendment, the state's house of representatives still had to vote. And those lawmakers weren't ready to make a decision. The vote got delayed over and over again. People on both sides kept talking with lawmakers, trying to win them over. A Tennessee journal wrote that in the heat of a discussion, one suffragist grabbed a lawmaker's tie and wouldn't let him go. Eventually, he took a knife from his pocket, cut himself free, and left.

Anti-suffragists were making their case all summer, too. Among them were Laura Clay and Kate Gordon, who'd worked alongside Carrie Chapman Catt in NAWSA just a year earlier. But now Clay and Gordon were fighting *against* the suffrage amendment. Clay and Gordon wanted the right to vote, but they didn't want Black women to have that right, too. When NAWSA's leaders wouldn't agree with them, Gordon and Clay left the group, stopped working for suffrage, and put all their energy into fighting the amendment.

While all this was going on—while everyone was sweating and arguing and waiting for the house to vote—Carrie Chapman Catt wrote a letter to her friend Mary Peck to share how frustrated she felt.

I've been here a month. It is hot, muggy, nasty, and this last battle is desperate.

Three days after she wrote that letter, things finally started happening. It was time for the house to vote.

The suffragists sat in the chamber, wearing yellow roses. The anti-suffragists were there, too, with red roses. They all held their breath and hoped the vote would go their way.

When the roll call began, most lawmakers who were expected to vote yes voted yes. Most who were expected to vote no voted no. It was so close that the whole thing came down to one vote.

That vote belonged to a young lawmaker named Harry Burn. Harry was from a rural area where most people didn't support the suffrage amendment. Lots of people thought he would vote no.

But when Harry's name was called, he voted yes.

Harry Burn voted *yes*!

It took a few minutes to sink in. The fight was over. The amendment would be ratified. Finally, women would have the right to vote! Supporters cheered, and yellow rose petals flew like confetti.

What made young Harry Burn vote yes? His mom. That's what he told the newspapers. She'd written him a letter that arrived before the vote that morning.

Hurrah and vote for suffrage and don't keep them in doubt. . . . I've been waiting to see how you stood but have not seen anything yet. Don't forget to be a good boy and help Mrs. Catt. . . .

With lots of love,
Mama

It turns out that Harry's mom, Phoebe Ensminger Burn, had been following all the drama in Nashville. She'd been watching the newspapers to see where her son stood on the suffrage amendment but hadn't seen his name mentioned. So she decided she should write him that letter, just to make sure.

I KNEW THAT A MOTHER'S ADVICE IS ALWAYS SAFEST FOR HER BOY TO FOLLOW AND MY MOTHER WANTED ME TO VOTE FOR RATIFICATION.

The people who had been fighting against suffrage didn't stop fighting. They tried to get the vote over-turned, but that didn't work. The amendment was ratified, and it was front-page news across the nation. Alice Paul added the last star to her ratification flag and unfurled it from the National Woman's Party's suffrage headquarters.

Can you guess what the suffragists did then?

They celebrated. Oh, did they celebrate! All over America, church bells rang out. There were parades and parties. After the celebration was over, the suffragists ran training sessions to teach women how to be active in politics. When it came time for the election of 1920, about 27 million American women had the right to vote.

Carrie Catt and her partner, Mollie Hay, voted at the polling place near their Manhattan apartment.

Alice Paul voted near her home in New Jersey. After all those pickets and hunger strikes, she could finally cast her ballot!

But not all women showed up to vote. Only about a third of eligible women chose to vote, a turnout that was disappointing for suffragists.

Why wouldn't everyone vote who could? The truth is, some women still didn't want to vote or weren't interested in politics, so they simply didn't show up. Others stayed home because their husbands didn't want them voting. There were issues with registration, too. In Mississippi and Georgia, women couldn't vote because their states had refused to extend the deadlines for them to register, even after the Nineteenth Amendment was ratified.

But for those who did vote—the women who'd been waiting and waiting and waiting for that moment—November 2, 1920, was a day they'd never forget.

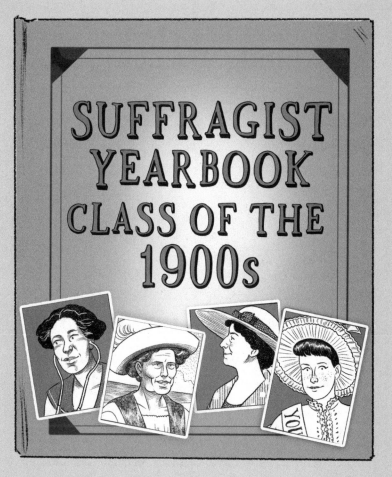

SUFFRAGIST
YEARBOOK
CLASS OF THE
1900s

Carrie Chapman Catt, Anna Howard Shaw, and Alice Paul are the names best known in the suffrage movement of the 1900s. But there's no way the movement would have succeeded without many other women—all with different talents and roles.

Most Likely to Be a Doctor/Trailblazer

VERINA MORTON-JONES graduated from medical school in 1888 and became the first woman licensed to practice medicine in Mississippi. In the early 1900s, she moved to Brooklyn, where she became president of the Brooklyn Equal Suffrage League. Morton-Jones also served as a board member on the National Association for the Advancement of Colored People from 1913 to 1925. She spent her life fighting racial discrimination and encouraging voter education.

The Woman-in-the-House Award

JEANNETTE RANKIN was one of the suffragists who had worked hard to win women the right to vote in Montana. But she wasn't finished with politics after that victory. Rankin was elected to the US Congress, and in 1917, she took her seat in the House of Representatives. She was the first woman to serve in Congress.

Island Suffragist Award

WILHELMINA KEKELAOKALANINUI WIDE-MANN DOWSETT was a Native Hawaiian woman who worked for women's suffrage even before Hawaii became a state. She organized Hawaii's first suffrage club in 1912, mostly made up of Native women who wanted the right to vote on issues in their territory. Wealthy white women in Hawaii were less likely to support the movement because they didn't want nonwhite voters to have power.

Dowsett argued that if women won the vote, they'd cast their ballots intelligently and honestly—and would probably end up being better voters than men.

The Youngest-Delegate Award

The youngest person sent as a delegate to represent other women at NAWSA's 1900 convention was a Radcliffe College student named MAUD WOOD PARK. She worked with a friend to organize the College Equal Suffrage League, to get even more young women involved in the movement.

The Creative-Solutions Award

Before **INEZ MILHOLLAND** rode her white horse to lead that big Washington, DC, suffrage parade, she'd done other work to rally young suffragists. When Harriot Stanton Blatch was organizing her open-air meetings, Milholland tried to make arrangements for a suffrage talk at Vassar College, where she was a student. Back then Vassar was an all-women's college. But when Inez Milholland asked for permission to bring in speakers about women's rights, the college's male president said no way. There would be no talk of woman suffrage on *his* campus. Milholland wasn't intimidated. She led a group of women into the cemetery next door to campus, and the traveling suffragists gave their talks there instead.

Most Likely to Spread the Word About Suffrage

When **FLORENCE LUSCOMB** was a little girl, she heard Susan B. Anthony speak and was inspired by her views. Luscomb grew up to study architecture at the Massachusetts Institute of Technology (MIT). She volunteered to sell copies of the *Woman's Journal*. She stood on Boston street corners, hawking newspapers in the rain and wind and snow to spread the message that women should have the right to vote.

The Winning-Washington Award

In 1910, Washington became the first state in fourteen years to approve woman suffrage. The victory was partly thanks to a Washington suffragist named EMMA SMITH DEVOE. She was a great speaker who understood her state. She realized that the controversial tactics being used on the East Coast—those loud public meetings and parades—might not work out so well in Washington. Instead, she and other organizers spoke at church meetings and farmers' granges, asking people to "give women a square deal." It worked. When men in Washington voted, they approved woman suffrage by almost a two-to-one margin.

WHAT'S THE BIG DEAL ABOUT SUSAN B. ANTHONY?

After reading about all those amazing women, you might be wondering why you haven't heard of more of them. If there were so many women working for suffrage, why do we hear about the same few ladies all the time? Why does Susan B. Anthony, for example, have her face on a coin, when nobody else does?

The answer to that question has to do, in part, with who wrote the history of the woman suffrage movement. Can you guess who might have done that?

If you guessed Susan B. Anthony, you're right.

In the 1880s, she and Elizabeth Cady Stanton started collaborating to write the official history of the woman suffrage movement. You might be looking at that date and thinking, *How could they write the official history when*

it would still be decades before women had the right to vote? That's what other suffragists were asking, too. Lucy Stone told Anthony and Stanton they should wait and write their history *after* women actually won the right to vote. Because, seriously, how could you write a complete history of something that was still in progress?

But Anthony and Stanton said that enough had already been accomplished to make the final victory a sure thing. They plowed ahead and wrote their multivolume project, called *History of Woman Suffrage*. They worked on it for years at Stanton's house, collecting newspaper articles, letters, and speeches. They wrote and rewrote, and finally they finished the first volume.

They had trouble finding a publisher, so Susan B. Anthony invested some of her own money to get the book published. When the first volume came out, she gave away hundreds of copies to libraries to make sure the history of the movement was shared. She didn't want the story told by someone else after she was gone; she wanted her version to be the official book on woman suffrage.

The plan worked. For years and years, Anthony and Stanton's *History of Woman Suffrage* was accepted as the one true story of the suffrage movement. Today, historians recognize that Anthony and Stanton's project shared a lot of detailed history but also that it sometimes emphasized their roles over others' contributions. Their version of the suffrage story left out a whole lot of people, including almost all the women of color who fought for the right to vote.

TEN
THE FIGHT GOES ON

The ratification of the Nineteenth Amendment was a huge victory for woman suffrage. But the fight for voting rights didn't end in 1920. Not by a long shot.

The Nineteenth Amendment didn't give voting rights to Native people or Chinese American people, who faced discriminatory laws back then. In parts of the South, governments did everything they could to make sure only white people got to vote. All kinds of tricky laws were passed to keep Black people from exercising their rights.

You might hope that would prompt an outcry from all those suffragists who had worked so hard to earn the vote. But you can probably guess by now that it didn't. They mostly left the Black women who'd fought alongside them all those years to keep fighting on their own. Those women—and their children—would play another leading role in the next battles for voting rights.

Native men and women won the right to vote when the Indian Citizenship Act was passed in 1924, but they still faced discrimination in many western states. In 1943, the government repealed, or got rid of, the Chinese Exclusion Act, which had kept people of Chinese ancestry from voting. But there was still no national law that truly guaranteed voting rights for everyone.

Forty years after the Nineteenth Amendment was passed, Black college students launched a huge voter registration campaign. One of its leaders was Ella Baker, a small young woman with a powerful voice. She wasn't afraid to speak up about injustice.

In 1960, Baker brought students together to form a new organization called the Student Nonviolent Coordinating Committee (SNCC, or "Snick"). Baker was a

leader in the new group and a mentor to other young Black women like Diane Nash and Bernice Johnson Reagon, who would continue the fight to empower all citizens.

So what's the big deal with voter registration? Generally, it involves filling out a form by a certain date, and that's it. But for Black people in the 1950s and 1960s, registering to vote could be difficult and dangerous, especially in the South. There, many states set up barriers to deny Black people the vote. Some required deliberately confusing literacy tests or high fees. There were even physical threats and intimidation.

SNCC students and activists created Freedom Schools to teach Black citizens about their rights and their history. SNCC recruited white volunteers and interracial teams to travel by bus on Freedom Rides from the Northern states to the South to help Black citizens register to vote. Their efforts were met with protest and often extreme violence.

But the activists pressed on. Student activist Lucretia Collins said the Freedom Rides had to continue, no matter what.

In 1962, Fannie Lou Hamer heard about voting from SNCC workers. She was a farmer who loved reading, even though she'd been forced out of school after only six years of education. She wanted to vote, even knowing there was reason to be afraid.

BUT WHAT WAS THE POINT OF BEING SCARED? THE ONLY THING THE WHITES COULD DO WAS KILL ME, AND IT SEEMED LIKE THEY'D BEEN TRYING TO DO THAT A LITTLE BIT AT A TIME SINCE I COULD REMEMBER.

Hamer was one of a group of eighteen citizens who tried to register to vote at a Mississippi courthouse. Armed white men patrolled the grounds, but she walked right in, ready to fill out the forms. Election officials gave her those phony literacy tests designed to prevent Black people from registering to vote. They declared that she'd "failed" and could not vote. Hamer promised she'd be back.

When she went home that day, she was fired from her job for her attempt to vote. Later a white mob shot at her and beat her so brutally that her vision and kidneys were permanently damaged. But she went on to help other Black people claim their right to vote.

In 1963, President John F. Kennedy, who had slowly come to support civil rights, asked the nation to consider how unjust it was being.

THE HEART OF THE QUESTION IS—WHETHER ALL AMERICANS ARE TO BE AFFORDED EQUAL RIGHTS AND EQUAL OPPORTUNITIES.

The following year, President Lyndon Johnson signed into law the Civil Rights Act of 1964. Part of that law made it illegal for employers to discriminate against people based on "race, color, religion, sex, or national origin."

This was followed by the Voting Rights Act of 1965. Even though Congress had passed voter protection laws before, states had continued to put up barriers, making it hard for people of color to vote. For the most part, the Voting Rights Act of 1965 changed that. With this strengthening of the Fifteenth Amendment, the federal government could approve or refuse states' changes to their voting laws. Many hoped for a big difference in Black votes and representation in government. And Black women continued to make their voices heard.

"DON'T DO ME ANY FAVORS . . ."

TRUE FEMINISM . . . DEMANDS EQUALITY BUT IT ALSO REQUIRES A COMMITMENT TO IMPROVE THE HUMAN CONDITION OF ALL THE SISTERS.

SHIRLEY CHISHOLM, WHO WORKED FOR BOTH WOMEN'S RIGHTS AND RACIAL JUSTICE, RAN FOR PRESIDENT IN 1972. SHE REFUSED TO SEPARATE HER TWO IDENTITIES—AS A BLACK PERSON AND A WOMAN—WHEN SHE CAMPAIGNED.

I AM NOT THE CANDIDATE OF BLACK AMERICA, ALTHOUGH I AM BLACK AND PROUD.

I AM NOT THE CANDIDATE OF THE WOMAN'S MOVEMENT OF THIS COUNTRY, ALTHOUGH I AM A WOMAN, AND I AM EQUALLY PROUD OF THAT.

CHISHOLM WANTED TO RUN AGAINST THE REPUBLICAN PRESIDENT IN OFFICE,

RICHARD NIXON.

BUT FIRST SHE HAD TO WIN THE DEMOCRATIC PARTY'S NOMINATION. SHE WAS UP AGAINST FIVE WHITE MEN.

YOU MIGHT THINK THAT WITH A FIELD LIKE THAT, FEMINIST LEADERS WOULD THROW THEIR SUPPORT BEHIND CHISHOLM. BUT THAT'S NOT QUITE WHAT HAPPENED.

ACTIVIST AND <u>MS.</u> MAGAZINE FOUNDER GLORIA STEINEM WAS ONE OF THE LOUDEST VOICES IN THE FEMINIST MOVEMENT. SHE SAID SHE SUPPORTED CHISHOLM.

ERA NOW!

WOMAN POWER

BUT SHE ALSO SAID SHE SUPPORTED GEORGE MCGOVERN AS . . .

. . . THE BEST WHITE MALE CANDIDATE.

The fight for voting rights still isn't over. When the Voting Rights Act of 1965 was passed, many believed that states would finally be unable to prevent citizens from exercising their right to vote. But a 2013 US Supreme Court decision declared parts of that law unconstitutional. That let states pass laws making it harder for people to vote. Some states started requiring a photo ID if you wanted to vote. Some got rid of early voting opportunities or added new requirements for voter registration.

There are other limits on voting rights, too. In many states, citizens who have been convicted of a certain type of crime lose their right to vote forever, even after they have served their time in prison. These kinds of laws prevent more than 6 million Americans from voting.

VOTING RIGHTS HEROES

Every day, people continue to work hard to make sure all citizens can participate in America's democracy.

Michelle Obama cofounded the organization When We All Vote. The group works to increase awareness of the voter registration process and offers a website where citizens can find information (whenweallvote.org). The First Lady reminds people that voting is an opportunity to be empowered.

WHEN YOU DON'T VOTE, WHAT YOU'RE REALLY DOING IS LETTING SOMEBODY ELSE TAKE POWER OVER YOUR OWN LIFE.

Groups like Color of Change and the Florida Rights Restoration Coalition have fought to restore voting rights to more than a million people who committed crimes in that state and served their time.

When the new law took effect, people like Robert Eckford of Florida, who hadn't been able to vote for years, were finally able to register to make their voices heard in the next election.

In Georgia, Stacey Abrams launched a voting rights organization called Fair Fight Action after she ran for governor in a controversial 2018 race. Some people challenged her white male opponent's win, partly because of a large number of uncounted votes in Black communities. Fair Fight Action is calling for changes in how elections are run, to make sure every voice is heard.

EVERY VOTE SHOULD BE COUNTED FROM EVERY CORNER OF OUR STATE.

Just as women like Mary Church Terrell and Josephine St. Pierre Ruffin did before them, members of groups like Black Voters Matter Fund and Woke Vote often work together to empower Black voters and promote justice in the democratic process.

WE'RE SHOWING PEOPLE THAT THEIR VOICE, THEIR ACTIVISM, THEIR UNDERSTANDING OF HOW THEIR COMMUNITIES WORK AND HOW THEY SHOULD WORK, IS REALLY WHAT'S IMPORTANT.

DeJuana Thompson,
Woke Vote

LaTosha Brown,
Black Voters Matter Fund

THE CHANGING FACE OF LEADERSHIP

Voting rights efforts throughout history have led to changes in who gets to run the country. America's 2018 elections were historic because citizens elected a much more diverse group of lawmakers than the nation had ever seen before, including a record number of women.

Deb Haaland (Laguna Pueblo) and Sharice Davids (Ho-Chunk Nation) became the first Native women in Congress.

Deb Haaland

Sharice Davids

Rashida Tlaib and Ilhan Omar became the first Muslim women elected to Congress.

Rashida Tlaib

Ilhan Omar

Texas sent its first Latina women to Congress.

Veronica Escobar

Sylvia Garcia

And for the first time, Massachusetts and Connecticut chose Black women to represent their states.

Ayanna Pressley

Jahana Hayes

White women made history as well. Tennessee and Arizona sent their first-ever female senators to Washington.

Marsha Blackburn

Kyrsten Sinema

Mississippi sent its first congresswoman, and Maine elected its first female governor.

Cindy Hyde

Janet Mills

Alexandria Ocasio-Cortez of New York became the youngest woman ever elected to Congress. She hopes many more young women will follow in her footsteps and run for office.

"We open doors so others can walk through them."

—ALEXANDRIA OCASIO-CORTEZ

Just imagine what all those women who fought for their right to vote would think if they could see their country now.

Alexandria Ocasio-Cortez

A WOMEN'S RIGHT-TO-VOTE TIMELINE

1769—American colonies have the same policy as the British, so married women can't own property in their own names. That means in most colonies women can't vote.

1787—The Constitutional Convention leaves voting rights up to states. All states except New Jersey decide women can't vote.

1807—Women lose the right to vote in New Jersey.

1839—Mississippi grants women the right to hold property in their own names if their husbands give permission.

1846—Women of Jefferson County, New York, submit a petition to the state legislature asking for the right to vote. (The legislature says no.)

1848—Elizabeth Cady Stanton and other women organize the Seneca Falls, New York, convention to talk about women's rights.

1850—The first national women's rights convention is held in Worcester, Massachusetts.

1851—Sojourner Truth delivers what's now called the "Ain't I a Woman" speech at the Women's Rights Convention in Akron, Ohio.

1866—Frances Ellen Watkins Harper speaks at the National Women's Rights Convention.

1867—Kansas holds its first referendum on woman suffrage and a separate vote on Black suffrage. Both are defeated.

1868—The Fourteenth Amendment is ratified and defines citizens and voters as men.

1869—Women in the Wyoming Territory win the right to vote.

1870—The Fifteenth Amendment is ratified, guaranteeing men the right to vote regardless of race or former condition of servitude.

1872—Victoria Claflin Woodhull runs for president with the National Radical Reformers Party.

Susan B. Anthony is arrested for trying to vote, in a test of the Fourteenth Amendment.

1873—The US Supreme Court rules that states can prohibit married women from practicing law.

1878—The woman suffrage amendment is introduced in Congress for the first time. It says, "The right of citizens of the United States to vote shall not be denied or abridged by the United States or by any state on account of sex."

1880—Mary Ann Shadd Cary organizes the Colored Women's Progressive Franchise Association in Washington, DC.

1883—Women in the Washington Territory win the right to vote.

1886—The US Senate defeats the suffrage amendment.

1887—Voters in Argonia, Kansas, elect America's first woman mayor, Susanna Madora Salter.

Women in the Montana Territory win the right to vote.

1890—The state of Wyoming grants voting rights to women.

The National American Woman Suffrage Association (NAWSA) is formed.

1893—New Zealand becomes the first country to give women full suffrage.

1893—Colorado women win the right to vote.

1894—Women deliver a petition with more than half a million signatures to the New York State Constitutional Convention. The Convention votes against a suffrage amendment.

1896—Idaho women win the right to vote.

Utah women win the right to vote.

The National Association of Colored Women is established, and Mary Church Terrell serves as its president.

1900—All states have passed laws so married women can own property.

Carrie Chapman Catt becomes president of NAWSA.

1907—Inspired by the British, suffragists begin holding public parades and meetings in the United States.

1910—The state of Washington grants women the right to vote.

1911—California women win the right to vote.

Jovita Idár becomes the first president of La Liga Femenil Mexicanista (the League of Mexican Women).

1912—Women in Arizona, Kansas, and Oregon win the right to vote.

1913—Alice Paul organizes a giant suffrage parade in Washington, DC.

Women in the Alaska Territory win the right to vote.

Illinois women win the right to vote—but only for president.

Ida B. Wells-Barnett founds the Alpha Suffrage Club in Chicago.

1914—The Congressional Union splits from NAWSA.

Women in the states of Montana and Nevada win the right to vote.

1916—Jeannette Rankin is elected to represent Montana in the US House of Representatives and in 1917 becomes the first woman in Congress.

Carrie Chapman Catt introduces her "Winning Plan," a two-pronged effort to push for state suffrage votes and a national amendment.

1917—The National Woman's Party begins White House pickets, and many arrests follow.

Women in New York win the right to vote.

Women win the right to vote for president in Nebraska, North Dakota, Ohio, Indiana, and Rhode Island.

1918—Women in Michigan, Oklahoma, and South Dakota win the right to vote.

The woman suffrage amendment passes in the US House of Representatives but fails by two votes in the Senate.

1919—Women in Iowa, Maine, Minnesota, Missouri, Tennessee, and Wisconsin win the right to vote for president.

The US House and Senate pass the suffrage amendment.

1920—The Nineteenth Amendment is ratified.

1923—The Equal Rights Amendment is introduced: "Men and women shall have equal rights throughout the United States and every place subject to its jurisdiction." Thirty-eight states had to ratify the amendment, and that didn't happen for almost a hundred years, long after the deadline Congress had set for ratification, so the amendment is still up in the air.

1924—The Indian Citizenship Act gives Native people the right to vote, but many western states still won't let them.

1932—Hattie Wyatt Caraway becomes the first woman elected to the US Senate, representing Arkansas.

1933—Frances Perkins becomes America's first female cabinet member, as President Franklin Delano Roosevelt's secretary of labor.

1943—The Chinese Exclusion Act is repealed so that people of Chinese ancestry can be citizens and vote.

1946—Felisa Rincón de Gautier is elected mayor of San Juan, Puerto Rico, becoming the first woman mayor in an American capital city.

1952—The Immigration and Nationality Act, also known as the McCarran-Walter Act, gives all people of Asian ancestry the right to become citizens and vote.

Charlotta Bass becomes the first Black woman to run for vice president, with the Progressive Party.

1963—Congress passes the Equal Pay Act.

1964—Title VII of the Civil Rights Act of 1964 prohibits sex discrimination in employment and creates the Equal Employment Opportunity Commission.

1965—The Voting Rights Act outlaws discrimination and intimidation at polls, encouraging more African Americans to vote.

1972—Title IX of the Education Amendments prohibits sex discrimination in all aspects of education programs that receive federal support.

Shirley Chisholm seeks the Democratic Party's nomination for president.

1974—Congress passes legislation to outlaw housing discrimination and credit discrimination based on gender.

1975—The US Supreme Court rules that states can't exclude women from juries.

1980—Paula Hawkins of Florida becomes the first woman elected to the US Senate without having had a husband or father who served in government first.

1981—Sandra Day O'Connor is appointed to become the first woman on the US Supreme Court.

1982—The deadline to ratify the Equal Rights Amendment passes without its being ratified.

1984—Geraldine Ferraro is the first woman nominated to be vice president on a major-party ticket.

Mississippi ratifies the Nineteenth Amendment.

1992—Many women are elected to Congress, with four winning Senate seats and twenty-four elected to first terms in the House of Representatives.

Carol Moseley Braun is the first Black woman elected to the US Senate.

1997—Madeleine Albright is appointed America's first woman secretary of state.

2007—Nancy Pelosi becomes America's first woman Speaker of the House.

2013—The ban on women serving in military combat positions is overturned.

2016—Hillary Clinton becomes the first woman to win a major political party's nomination to run for president.

2017—Nevada votes to ratify the Equal Rights Amendment.

2018—Illinois votes to ratify the Equal Rights Amendment.

A record number of women are elected to Congress.

2020—Virginia becomes the thirty-eighth of thirty-eight states to ratify the Equal Rights Amendment. However, because it came after the deadline Congress had set for ratification, the fate of the amendment is still up in the air. There will likely be more fights in courts and in Congress about whether the amendment will finally pass.

AUTHOR'S NOTE

When I was growing up in Western New York, most everyone knew Seneca Falls as the birthplace of women's rights. The summer after I graduated from high school, I took a road trip to the Finger Lakes with some girlfriends and visited the Women's Rights National Historical Park, where we read all about Elizabeth Cady Stanton and Susan B. Anthony. But it wasn't until I was much older that I heard other stories about the suffrage movement, including those that paint Stanton and Anthony in a less heroic light and those that celebrate other leaders in women's rights whose work was often ignored and whose stories were erased at the time.

Now that I'm all grown up and get to vote myself, I'm grateful for the work they all did to win the vote, just as I'm thankful for the work that modern voting rights advocates do in our world today. America's democracy is so much stronger when everyone has a voice.

I'm grateful to all the readers, librarians, and experts who helped with my research for this book and to Random House for helping me bring these stories to life. When we know the truth about our history and our democracy—even the parts that might not make us proud—we can all be better participants in that democracy and work together to make it stronger.

If you're reading this book right now, there's a good chance that you're not yet old enough to vote, but I bet you're looking forward to the day when you can. Don't ever forget what an important job it is. I'll be cheering for you when you get to cast that first ballot!

For now, if you'd like to learn more about the suffrage movement and voting rights, here are some books, websites, and museums you might like to check out.

BOOKS

Around America to Win the Vote: Two Suffragists, a Kitten, and 10,000 Miles by Mara Rockliff and Hadley Hooper (Candlewick, 2016)

Bold & Brave: Ten Heroes Who Won Women the Right to Vote by Kirsten Gillibrand and Maira Kalman (Knopf, 2018)

Voice of Freedom: Fannie Lou Hamer: The Spirit of the Civil Rights Movement by Carol Boston Weatherford and Ekua Holmes (Candlewick, 2015)

Votes for Women! American Suffragists and the Battle for the Ballot by Winifred Conkling (Algonquin, 2018)

With Courage and Cloth: Winning the Fight for a Woman's Right to Vote by Ann Bausum (National Geographic, 2004)

WEBSITES

African American Women Leaders in the Suffrage Movement: suffragistmemorial.org/african-american-women-leaders-in -the-suffrage-movement

Between Two Worlds: Black Women and the Fight for Voting Rights: nps.gov/articles/black-women-and-the-fight-for-voting-rights.htm

National Women's History Museum: womenshistory.org

StoryCorps, "A More Perfect Union": storycorps.org/animation/a-more-perfect-union

MUSEUMS TO VISIT

Belmont-Paul Women's Equality National Monument (Washington, DC)

Mary McLeod Bethune Council House (Washington, DC)

National Museum of African American History and Culture (Washington, DC)

Women's Rights National Historical Park (Seneca Falls, New York)

BIBLIOGRAPHY

Adams, Katherine H., and Michael L. Keene. *Alice Paul and the American Suffrage Campaign*. Urbana, IL: University of Chicago Press, 2008.

Bacon, Margaret Hope. *Valiant Friend: The Life of Lucretia Mott*. New York: Walker, 1980.

Baker, Jean H. *Votes for Women: The Struggle for Suffrage Revisited*. New York: Oxford University Press, 2002.

Bowean, Lolly. "9 Things You Must Know About Ida B. Wells-Barnett." *Chicago Tribune,* July 20, 2018. chicagotribune.com/news/ct-met -idabwells-nine-things-to-know-20180719-story.html.

Brown, DeNeen L. "Civil rights crusader Fannie Lou Hamer defied men—and presidents—who tried to silence her." *Washington Post,* October 6, 2017. washingtonpost.com/news/retropolis /wp/2017/10/06/civil-rights-crusader-fannie-lou-hamer-defied -men-and-presidents-who-tried-to-silence-her.

Camhi, Jane Jerome. *Women Against Women: American Anti-Suffragism, 1880–1920*. Brooklyn, NY: Carlson Publishing, 1994.

Catt, Carrie Chapman, and Nettie Rogers Shuler. *Woman Suffrage and Politics: The Inner Story of the Suffrage Movement*. Seattle: University of Washington Press, 1969. (Originally published by Charles Scribner's Sons, 1923.)

CBS/AP. "Florida ex-felons can begin registering to vote as amendment takes effect." CBS News, January 8, 2019. cbsnews .com/news/florida-ex-felons-begin-registering-to-vote-as -amendment-4-takes-effect.

"Chinese Girl Wants Vote." *New York Tribune*. April 13, 1912. chroniclingamerica.loc.gov/lccn/sn83030214/1912-04-13/ed-1 /seq-3.

Dickerson, Caitlin. "Overlooked: Ida B. Wells Obituary." *New York Times*. nytimes.com/interactive/2018/obituaries/overlooked -ida-b-wells.

Dubois, Ellen Carol. *Harriot Stanton Blatch and the Winning of Woman Suffrage*. New Haven, CT: Yale University Press, 1997.

Dubois, Ellen Carol. "Taking the Law into Our Own Hands: Bradwell, Minor, and the Suffrage Militance in the 1870s." In Wheeler, *One Woman, One Vote*, 81–98.

Dubois, Ellen Carol. "Working Women, Class Relations, and Suffrage Militance: Harriot Stanton Blatch and the New York Woman Suffrage Movement, 1894–1909." In Wheeler, *One Woman, One Vote*, 221–244.

"Equal Suffrage Hotly Debated." *Honolulu Star-Bulletin*. Honolulu. April 25, 1913. p. 7. chroniclingamerica.loc.gov/lccn /sn82014682/1913-04-25/ed-1/seq-7.

Faderman, Lillian. *To Believe in Women: What Lesbians Have Done for America—A History*. Boston: Houghton Mifflin, 1999.

Ford, Linda. "Alice Paul and the Triumph of Militancy." In Wheeler, *One Woman, One Vote*, 277–294.

Ford, Linda. *Iron-Jawed Angels: The Suffrage Militancy of the National Woman's Party 1912–1920*. Lanham, NY: University Press of America, 1991.

Fowler, Robert Booth. *Carrie Catt, Feminist Politician*. Boston: Northeastern University Press, 1986.

Fowler, Robert Booth. "Carrie Chapman Catt, Strategist." In Wheeler, *One Woman, One Vote*, 295–314.

Giddings, Paula. *When and Where I Enter: The Impact of Black Women on Race and Sex in America*. New York: William Morrow, 1984.

Ginzberg, Lori D. *Elizabeth Cady Stanton: An American Life*. New York: Hill and Wang, 2009.

Gordon, Ann D., ed. *The Selected Papers of Elizabeth Cady Stanton and Susan B. Anthony: In the School of Anti-Slavery, 1840 to 1866*. Vol. 1. New Brunswick, NJ: Rutgers University Press, 1997.

Gordon, Ann D., ed. *The Selected Papers of Elizabeth Cady Stanton and Susan B. Anthony: Against an Aristocracy of Sex, 1866 to 1873*. Vol. 2. New Brunswick, NJ: Rutgers University Press, 2000.

Griffith, Elisabeth. *In Her Own Right: The Life of Elizabeth Cady Stanton*. Oxford: Oxford University Press, 1984.

Haag, Matthew. "The Equal Rights Amendment Was Just Ratified by Illinois: What Does That Mean?" *New York Times,* May 31, 2018. nytimes.com/2018/05/31/us/equal-rights-amendment-illinois .html.

Hellman, Judith. *The Road to Seneca Falls: Elizabeth Cady Stanton and the First Woman's Rights Convention*. Urbana: University of Illinois Press, 2004.

Hendricks, Wanda A. "Ida B. Wells-Barnett and the Alpha Suffrage Club of Chicago." In Wheeler, *One Woman, One Vote*, 263–275.

Irwin, Inez Haynes. *The Story of the Woman's Party*. New York: Harcourt, Brace, 1921. Project Gutenberg: gutenberg.org /files/56701/56701-h/56701-h.htm.

Jones, Nikole Hannah. "When Ida B. Wells Married, It Was a Page One Story." *New York Times*, January 23, 2017. nytimes.com /interactive/projects/cp/weddings/165-years-of-wedding -announcements/ida-wells-wedding.

Kerber, Linda. "Ourselves and Our Daughters Forever: Women and the Constitution, 1787–1876." In Wheeler, *One Woman, One Vote*, 21–36.

Kerr, Andrea Moore. "White Women's Rights, Black Men's Wrongs: Free Love, Blackmail, and the Formation of the American Woman Suffrage Association." In Wheeler, *One Woman, One Vote*, 61–79.

Keyssar, Alexander. *The Right to Vote: The Contested History of Democracy in the United States*. New York: Basic Books, 2000.

Landers, Jackson. "'Unbought And Unbossed': When a Black Woman Ran for the White House." Smithsonian.com, April 25, 2016. smithsonianmag.com/smithsonian-institution/unbought-and -unbossed-when-black-woman-ran-for-the-white-house.

Landsman, Gail H. "The 'Other' as Political Symbol: Images of Indians in the Woman Suffrage Movement." *Ethnohistory* 39, no. 3 (1992): 247–284. https://doi.org/10.2307/482299.

Lerner, Gerda, Ed. *Black Women in White America*. New York: Vintage Books, 1992.

Lumsden, Linda J. *Inez: The Life and Times of Inez Milholland*. Bloomington: Indiana University Press, 2004.

Marilley, Susan M. *Woman Suffrage and the Origins of Liberal Feminism in the United States, 1820–1920*. Cambridge, MA: Harvard University Press, 1996.

Menand, Louis. "How Women Got in on the Civil Rights Act." *New Yorker*, July 21, 2014. newyorker.com/magazine/2014/07/21 /sex-amendment.

Menkart, Deborah, Alana D. Murray, and Jenice L. Vien, eds. *Putting the Movement Back into Civil Rights Teaching*. Washington, DC: Teaching for Change, 2004.

Palmer, Beverly Wilson. *Selected Letters of Lucretia Coffin Mott*. Urbana: University of Illinois Press, 2002.

Paybarah, Azi. "N.Y. Today: The City Has Few Statues of Women. Here Comes Shirley Chisholm." *New York Times*, November 30, 2018.

Rauterkus, Cathleen Nista. *Go Get Mother's Picket Sign: Crossing Spheres with the Material Culture of Suffrage*. Lanham, MD: University Press of America, 2010.

Rossi, Alice. "A Feminist Friendship: Elizabeth Cady Stanton and Susan B. Anthony." In Wheeler, *One Woman, One Vote*, 45–60.

Shaw, Anna Howard, Letter to Harriet Laidlaw, August 16, 1917. Schlesinger Library Laidlaw Collection, Folder 160, Box 8.

Sherr, Lynn. *Failure Is Impossible: Susan B. Anthony in Her Own Words*. New York: Random House, 1995.

Sims, Anastasia. "Armageddon in Tennessee: The Final Battle Over the Nineteenth Amendment." In Wheeler, *One Woman, One Vote*, 333–352.

Stanton, Elizabeth Cady. *Eighty Years and More (1815–1897): Reminiscences of Elizabeth Cady Stanton*. New York: Source Book Press (reprinting of original 1898 London edition), 1970.

Stevens, Doris. *Jailed for Freedom*. New York: Boni and Liveright, 1920.

Streitmatter, Rodger. *Raising Her Voice: African-American Women Journalists Who Changed History*. Lexington: University Press of Kentucky, 1994.

Terborg-Penn, Rosalyn. "African American Women and the Woman Suffrage Movement." In Wheeler, *One Woman, One Vote*, 135–155.

Tetrault, Lisa. *The Myth of Seneca Falls: Memory and the Women's Suffrage Movement, 1848–1898*. Chapel Hill: University of North Carolina Press, 2014.

United States Senate Committee on the District of Columbia. *Women's Suffrage and the Police: Three Senate Documents*. New York: Arno Press and the *New York Times*, 1971.

Van Voris, Jacqueline. *Carrie Chapman Catt: A Life*. New York: The Feminist Press, 1987.

Wagner, Sally Roesch. *Sisters in Spirit: Haudenosaunee (Iroquois) Influence on Early American Feminists*. Summertown, TN: Native Voices, 2001.

Walkman, Michael. *The Fight to Vote*. New York: Simon & Schuster, 2016.

Weiss, Elaine. *The Woman's Hour: The Great Fight to Win the Vote*. New York: Viking, 2018.

Wheeler, Marjorie Spruill, ed. *One Woman, One Vote: Rediscovering the Woman Suffrage Movement*. Troutdale, OR: New Sage Press, 1995.

Wheeler, Marjorie Spruill, ed. *Votes for Women: Woman Suffrage Movement*. Knoxville: University of Tennessee Press, 1995.

IMAGE CREDITS

INDEX

HISTORY SMASHERS

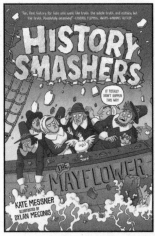

COMING SOON!

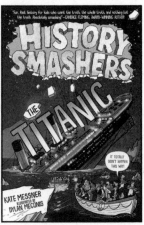